BILL GATES

THE PATH TO THE FUTURE

BILL GATES

THE PATH TO THE FUTURE

JONATHAN GATLIN

AVON BOOKS ◆ NEW YORK

AVON BOOKS, INC.
1350 Avenue of the Americas
New York, New York 10019

Copyright © 1999 by Bill Adler Books
Cover photograph by David Waite/LIAISON AGENCY
Published by arrangement with Bill Adler Books
ISBN: 0-380-80625-8
www.avonbooks.com

Library of Congress Cataloging in Publication Data:

Gatlin, Jonathan.
    Bill Gates : the path to the future / Jonathan Gatlin.
      p. cm.
    Includes bibliographical references (p.).
    1. Gates, Bill, 1955–   . 2. Businessmen—United States—Biography.
    3. Computer software industry—United States—History. 4. Microsoft
Corporation—History. I. Title.
    HD9696.63.U62G3744 1999   99-25008
    338.7'610053'092—dc21   CIP

First Avon Books Trade Paperback Printing: June 1999

AVON TRADEMARK REG. U.S. PAT. OFF. AND IN OTHER COUNTRIES, MARCA REGISTRADA,
HECHO EN U.S.A.

Printed in the U.S.A.

OPM   10 9 8 7 6 5 4 3 2 1

CONTENTS

BILL GATES
THE PATH TO THE FUTURE

CHAPTER ONE

THE BIGGEST DAY YET

In the United States, there's a willingness to let a young person start a company and hire people. The public, the press, and the marketplace often pay attention to the company's products, despite the youthfulness of the leader. If you prove to be surprisingly good at something while you're very young, many Americans put you in the "exceeds expectations" category. You've broken out of the ordinary mold and they wonder what you're capable of.

—BILL GATES, 1997

AUGUST 24, 1995

It would not rain on this day in Redmond, Washington, which was not far outside Seattle. Just in case, however, an enormous tent had been erected for the ceremony, scheduled for 11:00 A.M. Rain was an ever-present threat in the Seattle area, and it wouldn't do for the twenty-five hundred assembled guests to get wet. They included journalists from all over the world, the chief executive officers and technical geniuses from dozens of computer hardware and software manufacturers, political bigwigs, and even a surprise guest—Jay Leno of *The Tonight Show*. Hundreds of those in attendance were millionaires, including Leno, of course, and a very few were, like the host of this party, billionaires.

The host, William Henry Gates III, had organized this occasion to launch the latest and most important software product ever created by his company, Microsoft, which he had founded in 1975 at the age of nineteen with his boyhood friend Paul Allen. Allen left the company in 1984 after a serious bout with Hodgkin's disease, but he was still on the board, still a close friend, a billionaire in his own right, and very much present on this day of days, which was seeing the release of Windows 95, the most innovative upgrade yet of Microsoft's operating system for personal computers. Its predecessor, Windows 3.1, issued

Hardware and software companies strive to create products so attractive that consumers buy them even though they may already have similar, older products. This makes the upgrade business a powerful force for innovation. At Microsoft, for example, we knew we had to make Windows 95 dramatically better than Windows 3.1 or we would not get people to upgrade. We recognize that one of our toughest competitors is often the previous version of a product.

—BILL GATES, 1995

in 1991, was already installed on seventy-five million personal computers around the globe. The betting at Microsoft was that most of those computer users would want the new, improved version, with its fifteen million lines of code and numerous new features, including access to Microsoft's recently established Internet service. More than that, Windows 95 was expected to cause enough excitement that millions of people intrigued by the wild and wooly expansion of the Internet itself would purchase personal computers for the first time. Microsoft had predicted that it would sell thirty million copies of its new product in the first year. While that left the company's direct competitors grinding their teeth in envy and fury (many of them thought Windows 95, like its predecessor, would be far from the best possible technology), it was also the reason there were fourteen other, smaller tents on the vast Microsoft grounds that day. In those tents, computer manufacturers and software companies that had tailored their own new products to Windows 95 would be showing their wares to the assembled press.

Having predicted first-year sales of thirty million units, Microsoft was taking no chances in publicizing its new product. The hype had been going on for weeks. Bill Gates himself had given more than two dozen television interviews, from *Today* to *Larry King Live*. Gates had arranged with his friend Rupert Murdoch, owner of the *London Times*, to give away every copy of the newspaper printed on the day before the official Redmond party, with an ad proclaiming: "Window 95. Office 95. So good even The Times is complimentary." And in New York City, the Empire State Building was lighted up with Microsoft colors, red, yellow, and green. In Australia, Microsoft was giving five hundred dollars in cash to the first ninety-five babies

There's no shortage of competition in the computer industry. You'll never have anybody in a very dominant position for very long because they have to prove themselves constantly. You can't just sit on a market position; the fact that you have a seventy to eighty percent share means nothing in the next round.

—BILL GATES, 1993

born on August 24. This kind of publicity campaign needed a theme song that would resonate around the world. Bill Gates wanted the Rolling Stone song "Start Me Up," but the legendary rock group had never before allowed one of its songs to be used for commercial purposes. They made Microsoft pay big time for the privilege: several million dollars, with estimates on the price running as high as $12 million. But, after all, that was just small change in a total publicity budget of a quarter of a billion dollars.

Windows 95 was to go on sale to the public at 12:01 A.M. on August 24, as that date arrived by stages around the globe. Computer stores in major cities around the world opened their doors at midnight to accommodate the expected rush of those who couldn't wait until daylight to get their hands on the latest wonder of the computer world. According to James Wallace, author of *Overdrive*, the very first copy was sold in the not very big city of Auckland, New Zealand, to a business student. Reuters, the international news service, reported that a woman in Chicago, Illinois, said, "For computer people, this is their Woodstock." In New York City, a single Comp USA store had nine hundred people waiting in line at the magic hour.

As for the celebration under the tent in Redmond, Washington, that was a great success, too. When, in 1993, Bill Gates's engagement to Melinda French was announced, Jay Leno noted the event in his monologue by posing the question, "What's Bill Gates like after sex?" His answer: "Micro soft." But here Leno was in Redmond, being paid a handsome sum to tease Bill Gates some more by noting that he'd gone over to Gates's house and found the VCR blinking 12:00—some technical genius, that Gates. The crowd loved it and so, from all signs, did Gates. He might be worth $20 billion (and Windows 95 would help to al-

Much more recently, I've concluded that the wild success of the Internet signals a massive structural change in the computer and communications industries. I have long expected computer networks to achieve historic importance, but it has only been in recent months that I've come to expect the Internet to become mainstream. . . . This sea change is prompting us to critically reevaluate our plans—short-term and long-term. One of our highest priorities has become building Internet support into Windows, for example.

—BILL GATES, a month before the launch of Windows 95, July 1995

most double that amount within two years), but he always seemed to have a sense of humor.

In fact, Bill Gates was very tired. Some friends would later suggest that on that August day in 1995 he was on the verge of exhaustion. Within a couple of weeks, he and his wife, along with a group of friends, including fellow billionaire Warren Buffett and his wife, would take a two-week nonworking vacation in China, playing bridge as their train crossed the spectacular landscape to the famed Great Wall. Gates had every reason to be tired, despite his already legendary workaholic habits, which in earlier years had often meant sleeping under his desk. The release of Windows 95 had originally been scheduled for two years earlier, but numerous technical problems, along with the unexpected rise of the Internet—a turn in the road that Gates almost missed entirely—had twice delayed its launch. In addition, Gates had spent the last five years fending off extremely close antitrust scrutiny by the federal government.

But the biggest day yet had finally come. Beyond the tents on the emerald green grass of the Microsoft campus, a Ferris wheel had been installed, adding a gaudy note to the festivities. But there was plenty to celebrate, after all. As the Microsoft press pack revealed, even before the launch of Windows 95, sales of Windows 3.1 and its associated software had reached the point where somebody, somewhere on the planet, was using a newly purchased Windows product on the average of every 1.5 seconds.

CHAPTER TWO

A NEW WORLD BECKONS

Multimedia tools won't replace teachers and parents any more than textbooks do, nor will they make reading any less important than it is today. But pictures and sounds add immensely to the educational experience. I'm always an optimist. I believe kids growing up with access to these resources will retain more of their curiosity in adulthood. It makes me a little envious. Sometimes I get mail from kids telling me they want to be like me when they grow up. But when I look at what's going to be possible in the next few years, I wish I were a kid growing up now.

—BILL .GATES, 1995

Unlike such earlier giants of capitalism or innovation as Andrew Carnegie or Thomas Edison, Bill Gates was born, in 1956, into upper-middle-class comfort. His father, William Henry Gates II, was a highly successful lawyer, and his mother, Mary, the daughter of a banker, served on the boards of educational institutions, charities, and banks. Their Seattle home, with a view of Lake Washington, was large and comfortable, and their three children—Kristi, older by a year than Bill, and Libby, nine years younger— were given every advantage.

Bill Gates gives his parents a lot of credit for their style of raising their children and says that he hopes to emulate their blend of openness and discipline in bringing up his own children. But he himself was not an easy child to raise. It has been widely reported that by the time he entered sixth grade, young Bill had become so rebellious, particularly toward his mother, that he was put into counseling. Gates says that he enjoyed the experience, in part because the counselor gave him psychology books that were quite advanced for a twelve-year-old. Being treated like a grown-up apparently helped Bill calm down to some extent, but at the end of a year of sessions, according to *Time*, the psychologist bluntly told Mary Gates there was no use in trying to control her son; he was too competitive, and Mary would have to do the adjusting. In fact, some adjusting clearly took place on both sides, as Bill grew up to be very close to his mother.

Beginning with junior high, young Bill Gates was enrolled at the Lakeside School, a private school in Seattle. He was, in the words of his father, "small and shy," and it was also felt that a private school would be better able to respond to his very active intellectual needs. It was at the Lakeside School that Gates met Paul Allen, with whom

It's valuable to understand how the computer works, just to know what it can do and what it can't do. It's not able to learn, not like people do, where it picks up patterns and just gets smarter and smarter. A computer does exactly what we tell it to do. That's what programming is all about. If we tell it to do something stupid, that's exactly what it will do. It will keep on doing it and it won't have any idea that it's doing the wrong thing.

—BILL GATES, explaining the computer to children on a
Linda Ellerbee Nickelodeon special, April 1997

he would found Microsoft only seven years later. At the time they met, Gates was twelve, Allen two years older. As Gates acknowledges, it is unusual for boys that age to become friends when more than a year separates them, but they shared a number of interests; in particular, both boys were fascinated by the computer terminal that was bought for the school by its Mother's Club, which also raised money to buy computer time on a mainframe. The terminal didn't even have a screen. The students had to wait for answers to come clacketing out of a noisy printer.

Using the terminal, Gates wrote his first program at the age of thirteen. It was only a computerized tic-tac-toe game that could have been played much more rapidly with pencil and paper, but the boys were already entranced with the sense of power that came from making a machine carry out their commands. Gates, Allen, and a third boy, Kent Evans, who was Bill Gates's best friend, formed the Lakeside Programmers Group. This grown-up sounding name helped them get an actual spare-time job writing a payroll system for a small Seattle company. They were learning to become businessmen at a very young age, but they were also soon confronted with an adult-level tragedy: Kent Evans was killed in a mountain climbing accident. Gates has said that for "two weeks I couldn't do anything at all."

In the aftermath of Kent Evans's death, Gates and Allen became even closer. There was a playful side to some of their collaborations, including writing a program for playing the board game Risk—although Gates's critics take pleasure in pointing out that the object of the game is world domination. But they were also learning—fast—and they put their ever-increasing expertise to use in a number of programming jobs for local firms. These ventures helped Bill Gates develop greater confidence, and he began to

It's well documented that there are people who can recall detailed information that they have only scanned and never really thought about. I'm certainly not one of them. I have a good memory, though, for information that I've been deeply involved with or have cared about. I can remember all the moves of many chess games that I've played. I can still remember all the lines in a high school play, *Black Comedy*. I was so afraid that I'd forget the lines that I just burned them into my head. I remember financial data very well, too.

—BILL GATES, 1996

demonstrate an increasing social poise, as well, which must have pleased his mother, who had that quality in abundance. Gates is particularly fond of recalling that he even was given the lead in a school production of Peter Shaffer's famous farce *Black Comedy*, taking a role originated at England's Chichester Festival by Tom Courtenay, the British actor most famous for his role in the movie *The Loneliness of the Long Distance Runner*. In one of his newspaper columns, Gates squelched the idea that he had a "photographic memory," but said that he still remembered all of his lines from *Black Comedy* twenty-five years later because he had been so afraid of forgetting them during performance that he had "burned them" into his head.

One job that he and Paul Allen had was a young hacker's dream. A company had bought a new computer that didn't have to be paid for until the bugs were eliminated. "The company saved money," Gates remembers, "by commissioning us to find ways to crash its system—fun for eager young programmers." Gates goes on to warn, however, that unauthorized attempts to do that today are criminal offenses. On another job that he and Allen and some other boys had, they were paid what he notes was an "extraordinary" amount for a teenage summer job—$5,000—although some of it was paid in computer time instead of cash. He found himself working on a program that scheduled classes for his own school, and by adding a "few instructions," he saw to it that he was almost the only boy in a class full of girls. In part it may have been this kind of stunt that causes some schoolmates to remember him less than fondly.

Both Gates and Allen, however, pinpoint the real start of their business collaboration as having taken place in the summer of 1972. In the magazine *Electronics*, way in the

BASIC didn't become the best-known and most accessible computer language just because it comes free with every machine. BASIC's strengths—the simplicity of using an interpreter, its powerful string handling, the richness of the language, its English-like keywords and syntax, and the freedom it gives programmers to experiment—make it the ideal way for computer novices to explore the intricacies of their computers.

—BILL GATES, on the twenty-fifth anniversary of BASIC, 1989

back pages, Paul Allen found an article about the Intel 8008 microprocessor chip. This was Intel's second chip, twice as powerful as the first one they had produced the year before, and Allen immediately realized that such chips would get more powerful quickly. Indeed, in 1965 Intel cofounder Gordon Moore had predicted that chips would double in capacity every year. This prediction came true, and by the late 1970s, engineers were referring to Moore's Law.

Gates and Allen ordered an Intel 8008 chip the summer of 1972, paying $360 for it. Gates had thought he could work out a form of BASIC (Beginner's All-purpose Symbolic Instruction Code) to run on the 8008 chip, but he discovered it just wasn't powerful enough; it didn't contain enough transistors yet. But they were able to use the chip to run a program they developed for traffic-volume-count analysis, and they envisioned selling computers for that purpose. To do so they formed their first company, called Traf-O-Data. Paul Allen notes that the company "wasn't a roaring success." Their prototype machine, although it worked well enough, attracted no buyers; the fact that its designers were teenagers probably didn't help. The boys did get a few customers to make use of the program itself, but the most important aspect of Traf-O-Data was that it gave them some real business experience.

Allen had graduated Lakeside School and was going to Washington State University. Gates did much of the writing of the Traf-O-Data program while traveling across the state by bus to confer with his friend and business partner. Allen was bored by college and wanted to form a new company as soon as Gates graduated in 1973—a company with a broader purpose than Traf-O-Data's. But Gates's parents insisted that he enroll at Harvard; he had been getting top marks since the ninth grade, when he had

It's considered cool these days to be wired into the worlds of computers and communications, but I'm not sure anyone wants to be thought of as a "nerd." If being a nerd means you're somebody who can enjoy exploring a computer for hours and hours late into the night, then the description fits me, and I don't think there's anything pejorative about it. But here's the real test: I've never used a pocket protector, so I can't really be a nerd, can I?

—BILL GATES, 1996

"decided to get all As without taking a book home," as he puts it. When he placed within the top ten in the country on a math aptitude test, his rebellious period ended.

Much has been made of the fact that at Harvard Bill Gates did "unconventional" things like going to the lectures for classes he wasn't taking instead of the ones he was. But in fact this kind of behavior was not all that peculiar at Harvard. Students were expected to attend small seminar-type classes where student discussion was important, but otherwise it was the grades that counted, not class attendance or study habits. Gates has admitted that his habit of procrastinating until the last moment before an exam and then cramming frantically was not a good precedent for running a business.

In the fall of 1974, Gates's sophomore year, Paul Allen drove across country in his old Chrysler and took a job programming for Honeywell, located near Boston. That meant he and Gates could brainstorm to their hearts' content about the future of computers and the place they were now sure they would have in that world. But the letters they sent out netted them very little interest. Then, just before Gates flew home for Christmas, the January 1975 edition of *Popular Electronics* came out. The two friends perused it while standing in the freezing cold at the Harvard Square newsstand. The cover was topped by the following headline: "Project Breakthrough! World's First Microcomputer Kit to Rival Commercial Models . . . 'Altair 8800' Save over $1000."

Altair was a distant star that had come to be known to millions because it had been visited by the starship *Enterprise* in a *Star Trek* episode. The two young men saw that the Altair was little more than a toy with switches and blinking lights, since it had no keyboard or display panel,

I had done a lot of work after the age of thirteen studying microsoftware and I became a fantastic developer, but I kept asking great developers to look at my code and show me where it could be better, how it could be different. I'd move to a new level. When Microsoft started, there was a lot of camaraderie of challenging each other: "Can you tighten up this code? Can you make this better?" It was an era of great craftsmanship. It was a different world.

—BILL GATES, *In the Company of Giants,* by RAMA DEV JAGER and RAFAEL ORTIZ, 1997

and no software to run it. But they were taken aback to discover that it did have the new 8800 chip brought out by Intel the previous spring, which was ten times as powerful as the 8008 they had used for their Traf-O-Data program. Their reaction was one of dismay that the future was already happening without them, that people would be writing genuine software for that chip, making the Altair 8800 something more than a toy after all. They didn't have either an Altair microcomputer or an 8800 chip. Paul Allen, as Gates writes in *The Road Ahead*, "studied a manual for the chip, then wrote a program that made a big computer at Harvard mimic the little Altair. This was like having a whole orchestra available and using it to play a simple duet, but it worked." The two then spent five exhausting, almost sleepless weeks writing a BASIC program for the Altair.

They then managed to persuade MITS, the manufacturer of the Altair, to sell their program. MITS was a very small company, located in out-of-the-way Albuquerque, New Mexico. But Gates and Allen didn't care; they were in on the ground floor of what they were convinced was the computer wave of the future. MITS offered Allen a job and gave the two young men space in their offices in a strip mall. Allen quit his job at Honeywell, and Gates took a leave from Harvard. He discussed the move thoroughly with his parents. Recognizing his ability and his intense desire to have his own company, they went along with their son's wishes. Leaving Harvard is something Gates still finds himself having to discuss regularly. It comes up in the numerous interviews he gives, and it has been a frequent subject of inquiry on the part of young computer whizzes sending questions for his newspaper column. Gates always points out that he enjoyed Harvard and dis-

I've always rejected the term *entrepreneur* because it implies that you're an entrepreneur first and a software creator second. I didn't say, "Oh, I'll start a company. What will it be? Cookies? Bread? Software? No. I'm a software engineer and I decided to gather a team together. The team grew over time, built more and more software products, and did whatever was needed to drive that forward. Entrepreneurship is to me an abstract notion.

—BILL GATES, *In the Company of Giants*, 1997

courages those who think they're smart enough to skip going just because he did. He emphasizes that his taking a leave was in large part a matter of timing—something brand new was happening that he was certain he could be an important part of. He is too modest—or too politic—to make the obvious statement that he had a special genius that not too many people possess. More broadly, he tries to indicate that he had quite broad interests and was already remarkably well educated in the liberal arts.

Both Gates and Allen had some savings when they started out. Allen had made good money at Honeywell. Gates, in addition to what he had earned as a programmer during the past few summers, had managed to amass a fair amount of money playing poker at Harvard, a fact he seems almost boyishly proud of. At the time, of course, he was in some ways little more than a boy—only nineteen—and Allen was only two years older. Gates has duly noted that in many other countries, both the business world and the public at large are much less receptive to very young entrepreneurs than in the United States, and that he was fortunate to have been born an American, at just the right time for his abilities.

There is some confusion about which of the partners came up with the name Microsoft. Gates has said that he did, but Allen, even in joint interviews, sometimes gives the impression that the final decision was his. At the beginning, however, the name was a little different: Micro-Soft. Gates told *Fortune* that the credit line in the source code of their first product was "Micro-Soft BASIC: Bill Gates wrote a lot of stuff; Paul Allen wrote some other stuff." They had also considered calling the company Allen and Gates, but the example of IBM and others suggested that a more generic name was better in terms of a company's longevity, at

It may seem ironic, considering that I didn't get my degree, but Microsoft focuses its hiring for most positions on college graduates. We believe that the maturity and learning that a college education offers are invaluable, and we've seen that people with liberal arts educations bring wider knowledge of the world to bear on their jobs.

I've said it before and I'll say it again: "Go to college."

—BILL GATES, 1996

least in the computer world. Allen and Gates, they thought, sounded too much like a law firm. It was not until 1981 that they finally got around to incorporating as Microsoft.

In Albuquerque they continued to live much like college students, sometimes going to a movie but mostly working, often very late; Gates not only slept under his desk at the office but sometimes fell asleep in meetings. Allen, who would go home to their motel to sleep, often had to be routed out of bed with a phone call from Gates. Both men admit that they had to learn business practices as they went along. All decisions were made mutually, often after hours of discussion, but they agree that Allen was the one to take the lead in suggesting new products, while Gates was out in front on the business end. They both wrote code in those days, with Allen doing more of it but Gates showing a particular flair for solving knotty problems, as had always been the case.

The press has long reported that the relationship between Gates and Allen had a tendency to erupt into huge fights. That problem goes back to the very beginning. When they were still at Lakeside School, Allen tried to go it alone on a paid project, and then found that he needed Gates's coding input, after all. *Time* has reported that Gates replied, "OK, but I'm in charge, and I'll get used to being in charge, and it'll be hard to deal with me from now on unless I'm in charge." Although they encountered serious difficulties later, both men say that the Albuquerque days were relatively free of argument. In part this may have been because they were too excited and too busy to fight.

It took them a while to realize that the low bids they were using to ensure landing a contract with companies like Texas Instruments could be raised without fear. Most companies, it turned out, were willing to pay more than

Next door was a vacuum-cleaner place, then a massage parlor. To get to our offices, you had to walk past the vacuum-cleaner guy. We stayed in this motel down the road called Sand and Sage. We're talking real sage, not some hypothetical thing. Every morning all the cars in the parking lot had all this sagebrush and tumbleweed that blew underneath them.

—BILL GATES, recalling the early days for *Fortune*, 1995

they asked. They had bid $99,000 on a Texas Instruments job simply because they didn't quite have the guts to go to six figures. But they got over their shyness in that department quickly, as they realized that their competitors often simply couldn't manage to do the job as fast or as well.

At the same time, however, they also found themselves promising product they hadn't even developed yet, and having to play very serious catch-up. The Japanese company Ricoh once sent a man over just to sit in their offices and make sure they were working on an overdue project for Ricoh and not something else. By agreeing to develop software that they hadn't yet fully thought through, they not only pushed themselves to the limit but also challenged themselves in ways that kept them ahead of their competitors. There are critics of the computer industry in general today, and of Microsoft in particular, who say that the intensely competitive nature of the industry has led to a bad habit of overpromising and of hyping new features that are hardly a gleam in anyone's eye. Microsoft has often been accused of heralding new features not even in real development simply in order to scare off the competition. Some competitors say, "See, they were doing it even back in Albuquerque." But Microsoft denies that it does that today, and Gates and Allen point out that in the early days the software industry was so new that it was perfectly natural to ask a hardware manufacturer what they wanted and agree to provide it with only the sketchiest idea of how to fulfill the request. They were dealing with virgin territory, and exploring it often meant saying yes to something when the path through the woods wasn't yet clear. It was necessary to "hack" their way through in more ways than one.

Controlling expectations—whether about deliveries, product features, or stock value—is often wise in a technology business. It's a lot better to underpromise and overdeliver.

—BILL GATES, 1996

While there were certainly crises in terms of developing new software, the most frightening episode in the early history of Microsoft proved to be a business matter. The initial contract they had signed with MITS called for that company to sell the Gates/Allen BASIC to their customers, rather than Microsoft's selling it to computer owners and buyers directly. That seemed to be a smart move, since it cut down on the sales effort for Microsoft. But the contract only called for MITS to make a "best effort" to sell the software, and they soon stopped making almost any effort. The problem was that the Gates/Allen BASIC was being widely pirated, which mostly meant that people were getting the software from a friend.

The two partners went into arbitration to try to make MITS honor the contract. But the arbitration took nine months, and while it was taking place, MITS withheld payments from Microsoft. Gates and Allen say flatly that MITS was trying to "starve" them to death. As they couldn't even pay their lawyer, they almost accepted a settlement, but a decision to hold out paid off when the arbitrator finally came down foursquare on their side. Had they lost the arbitration, they would have had to begin all over again. Both say it was a very scary period, but in the end it taught them valuable business lessons about keeping control of their own destiny; future contracts had many safeguards built into them. Microsoft is often charged with being tough to the point of ruthlessness, but Gates and Allen learned the hard way that toughness was essential to survival.

Other companies had started entering the personal computer market, including Commodore and Radio Shack, but it was the Apple II that really took off. MITS, a small company with less vision and talent, had been left behind

If somebody had foreseen that personal computers were going to be a huge business, the obvious investment would have been in PC manufacturers. But the vast majority of PC manufacturers failed, although if you had happened to pick Compaq or a few others you would have done well.

—Bill Gates, on the risks of investing in the Internet, 1995

by the end of 1978. In addition, in 1978, Gates had entered into an agreement with a go-getting Japanese entrepreneur named Kazuhiko Nishi, or Kay. He had contacted Microsoft, and he and Gates, who were the same age, had hit it off immediately. Gates describes Kay in *The Road Ahead* as "flamboyant," something Gates himself never was but which he clearly appreciated in his new colleague. With Kay as a go-between, Microsoft was now doing almost half its business with Japanese companies. MITS was fading away, so there was no longer any reason to remain in Albuquerque. On the first day of 1979, Gates and Allen moved their business home to the Seattle area, settling into the suburb called Belvue. They had almost a dozen employees, and almost all of them made the transfer to the new base.

Ensconced in Seattle, the company grew quickly. By early 1980, there were thirty-five employees, and Gates and Allen knew they needed management help. It had become impossible for the two of them to spread themselves thin enough to review all the new code that was being written. Gates decided to turn to an old friend from his two-year Harvard career, Steve Ballmer. Ballmer had lived down the hall from Gates their sophomore year, and they had taken courses together in mathematics and economics. As Ballmer once told *Time*, Gates would "play poker until six in the morning, then I'd run into him at breakfast and discuss applied mathematics." Like so many others, Ballmer thinks Gates is the smartest man he's ever met. But he wasn't initially too sure he wanted to join Microsoft, at least right then. After Harvard he had joined Procter & Gamble as a product development manager, and then entered business school at Stanford University in California. He'd only finished one year when he was contacted by Gates, and thought he'd rather finish taking his degree. Gates asked

If you think you're a really good programmer, or if you want to challenge your knowledge, read *The Art of Computer Programming* by Donald Knuth. Be sure to solve the problems. . . . It took incredible discipline, and several months, for me to read it. I studied twenty pages, put it away for a week, and came back for another twenty pages. You should definitely send me a resume if you can read the whole thing.

—BILL GATES, 1995

his mother, a very persuasive woman, to talk to Ballmer, and clinched the deal by offering Ballmer part ownership of Microsoft. By 1995, Ballmer's percentage of the company was five percent, worth $2.7 billion, and the value of his shares has substantially increased since then.

Ballmer is credited by both Gates and impartial observers with having played a major part in the company's success, and in the years since Paul Allen's departure from Microsoft, Ballmer became increasingly close to Gates, serving as best man at Gates's January 1, 1994 wedding. But the beginning was somewhat rocky. After only three weeks of getting to know how Microsoft worked, Ballmer insisted that they needed to hire another seventeen people immediately and fifty within short order. Gates was horrified. He wanted the company to be "lean and hungry"; having seen other computer companies go bankrupt practically overnight, he wanted a cash cushion large enough that Microsoft could run for a year without any money coming in.

Ballmer was adamant about the need for new people. In addition, he was so angry at having his judgment questioned—right after being brought in to supposedly make just this kind of decision—that he moved out of the house he and Gates were sharing. Gates's father stepped in to calm things down, and Bill Gates relented, permitting the new hirings to go through. It was just as well that he did. The new people, and many more, would be needed soon.

CHAPTER THREE

THE RISE OF A JUGGERNAUT

The computer and software industries have thrived over the past twenty years precisely because there was little regulation of technical standards. . . . When the marketplace chooses standards, they aren't perpetually frozen. Competitors have incentives to innovate as they try to topple existing standards. It's a great system called capitalism. We need more of it, not less.

—BILL GATES, on the need for free markets, 1995

By 1980, the Apple II and other personal computers on the market were changing the minds of bigger, older computer companies about the future of the personal computer. IBM, which dominated the market for large mainframe computers, and Digital Equipment Corporation, which had been doing a booming business in what were then seen as "smaller" computers with a wide variety of applications, had been slow about seeing that PCs were the wave of the future. Indeed, Ken Olsen, the founder of DEC (whom Bill Gates had idolized as a teenager), had been debunking the PC since 1977, when he told a convention of The World Future Society, "There is no reason for any individual to have a computer in his home." This famously mistaken judgment meant that DEC would later have to make a massive attempt to catch up, and it eventually led to Olsen's ouster from the company.

IBM was also slow to see the possibilities of the PC, but at least it had the excuse that it was the leader in mainframes around the world. IBM was dubious, but not about to be caught entirely flat-footed, and in 1980 it made contact with Microsoft. It had a secret project for the development of PCs; if it was going to get them launched quickly, it would be necessary to go outside the company for the development of software to run the machines, rather than going through the lengthy process of trying to scale down its own mainframe software. Bill Gates had always been afraid that one of the big boys would do just that, leaving Microsoft in the dust. DEC had in fact scaled down some of its software in 1979, but because Olsen didn't really believe in PCs to begin with, the company hadn't gotten behind their new product in a way that threatened Microsoft.

IBM started off by playing things very cool. They sent

When IBM introduced its PC in 1981, many people attacked Microsoft for its role. These critics said that 8-bit computers, which had 64K of address space, would last forever. They said we were wastefully throwing out great 8-bit programming by moving the world to 16-bit computers.

—BILL GATES, when 32-bit systems were standard, 1996

two executives to Seattle, but as Gates would later tell the story, these men downplayed their own importance, saying that they were just planning people and much of what they planned never happened. But they had a long discussion with Gates and Allen about where the technology was headed, and the big prospects for personal computers. They said they would like to have Microsoft's FORTRAN and COBOL languages, and perhaps a good deal more. The meeting made Gates think back to their Albuquerque experience with Ricoh, when Microsoft had promised software it hadn't even developed yet.

But Microsoft had a possible ace in the hole this time. It was negotiating to buy a little-known system called Q-DOS from a small rival company called Seattle Computer. If they could get their hands on it soon enough, they could license it to IBM. With Kay Nishi, their Japanese cohort, pushing them forward, Microsoft found themselves offering Q-DOS to IBM before the final papers with Seattle Computer had been signed. Two days of agonizing suspense ensued, with Gates and Allen worrying that Seattle Computer would get wind of the IBM deal and greatly raise their price. But since IBM was itself trying to keep its PC project secret, word didn't leak, and Microsoft got Q-DOS for only $50,000. The system would prove instrumental in making Microsoft the industry giant it became.

Seattle Computer's Q-DOS underwent many changes, of course, before becoming Microsoft's MS-DOS. Microsoft had hired away the top engineer at Seattle Computer, Tim Paterson, and put him in charge of developing the new version. Since Microsoft also worked closely with IBM on the actual design of the IBM PC, there was a great deal of work to be done. Bill Gates and Paul Allen were still involved in hands-on development work, the actual creating

The weirdest thing of all, though, was when we asked to come to the big official launch of the PC in New York, IBM denied us. About four days later we got this form letter that IBM probably sent to every vendor, even the guy who had the capacitators in the machine. It said something like, "Dear vendor, thank you for your help, blah, blah, blah." They eventually apologized to us for that.

—BILL GATES, 1995

of code, in those days, and the tension that must have existed from 1980 to 1981 surfaced momentarily fifteen years later when the two men gave a joint interview to *Fortune*. In the interview, Gates brought up the fact that in the midst of the IBM project, Allen had insisted on going to see a space shuttle launch. Allen quickly put in that it was the *first* space shuttle launch and that he had gone down to Florida and flown back the same day, being absent less than thirty-six hours.

Originally designed for the Intel 8088 or 8086 microprocessing chips (and later for more advanced chips), MS-DOS was a powerful 16-bit operating system, using the then standard character-based mode that would be superseded by the graphical interface developed for the Macintosh three years later. The original MS-DOS had a memory limit of 640K, but that too would eventually be surpassed. Even with the advent of the graphical Windows operating system, MS-DOS continued to provide the underlying support. The initial MS-DOS system was considered fast, but as more powerful microprocessing chips were developed by Intel, it was updated to operate at much greater speed. A great deal of Microsoft's success can be attributed to the fact that in MS-DOS it created an operating system that could serve as a sound basis for succeeding generations of more sophisticated operating systems and endless software applications.

Although the IBM PC would be in direct competition with the Apple II, Microsoft also developed its first application for Apple Computer in 1980. This was the Softcard for Apple II, which allowed that computer to run the CP/M operating system of Digital Research. But at the time, it was the relationship with IBM that Gates and Allen saw as the central building block for the future. Microsoft was

It was great that Paul got better, and we wanted him to come back more than anything. But there was just no part-time way to come back to Microsoft. If you were going to be there, you were really going to work hard. We all knew that. It's still that way.

—BILL GATES, 1995

not paid a great deal for its development work for IBM—less than $200,000—but Gates made certain that their contract with IBM allowed for Microsoft's adapting MS-DOS for the clones of the IBM PC, which the hardware giant was prepared to authorize.

Once the IBM PC was on the market, Microsoft pushed MS-DOS hard, persuading other software companies to develop applications for the operating platform. This was important, since IBM was offering a choice of software, also making available a version of Digital Research's CP/M operating system, as well as a far more expensive UCSD Pascal P-System. Since Microsoft charged IBM only a one-time fee, the MS-DOS cost only $60, as opposed to $175 for the CP/M and $450 for the UCSD system. Gates and Allen were convinced that if they could establish MS-DOS as the system in greatest use, they could make a great deal of money down the line. Their gamble paid off, and MS-DOS won the battle within a year. What's more, the first clones were coming out, and Microsoft was poised to cash in. In addition, new software like the Lotus 1–2–3 spreadsheet was created to work with MS-DOS.

But just as Gates and Allen arrived at this moment of triumph, Allen was diagnosed with Hodgkin's disease. It was initially thought that he had lymphoma, an often fatal form of cancer, but even the treatment for the much more controllable Hodgkin's disease would entail twenty-two months of chemotherapy. Although he remained a director of Microsoft and sometimes attended various other meetings, Allen backed off from his commitment to Microsoft during the two years of treatment. When he recovered, he made the decision to go off on his own to do other things. By then he was already a billionaire several times over, and he proved himself to be an astute investor in other

Software companies are forced to gamble on unproved markets because it's nearly impossible to ask customers to predict whether they'll buy and use a new kind of tool. Successful software companies push the frontier of what's possible. We have no choice but to spend all the money to create a product before we sell any—and then hope there's a big market for it.

—BILL GATES, 1997

companies, ranging from Ticketmaster, of which he owns eighty percent, to America Online and many high-tech companies. He bought the NBA Portland Trailblazers and became one of the new owners of the Seattle Mariners, in order to keep the baseball team in Seattle. He gives millions of dollars to charity every year, the beneficiaries ranging from cancer and AIDS research to libraries and the Oregon Shakespeare festival. As a director of Microsoft, he still has official input into shaping the company, but it's clear that he has a special place as an informal prognosticator and sounding board for Bill Gates, and that the men remain both intellectually and personally close.

With Paul Allen no longer a major force at Microsoft after his illness struck in 1982, it was up to Bill Gates to continue to build the company into the worldwide behemoth it has become. There are those who say that Paul Allen is a nicer guy than Bill Gates, and that it wouldn't have been as ruthless a company if Allen had remained with it in his original capacity. But that ignores the fact that Gates was from the start more involved with the business end. And while Gates sometimes snaps back when charged with extreme aggressiveness, and denies many charges made against his company's business practices, it is obvious he has run it with enormous success.

The first big step Microsoft took without Allen's active participation was to develop a graphical interface. MS-DOS was character based. Gates explains the difference between the two formats by using a chessboard analogy: one format moves a chess piece by typing in words; the other shows a chessboard on the screen and moves the representation of the chess piece with a mouse. It may seem incredible to young computer users, but it was not until 1984 that the use of the mouse really became popular, with the introduc-

Our failures tend to result from markets being too small. Microsoft Bob was a product a couple of years ago that used on-screen cartoon characters to carry out tasks for people. Unfortunately, the software demanded more performance than typical computer hardware could deliver at the time and there wasn't an adequately large market. Bob died.

—BILL GATES, 1997

tion of Apple's Macintosh. The technology of the mouse had originally been developed by Xerox, but because of the high cost of their computers, which also didn't use standard microprocessors, they were unable to achieve market success with this breakthrough.

The Macintosh was a different matter entirely. Microsoft's reputation was such that Apple developed the Macintosh working closely with Gates's company. Microsoft's first graphical products, the word processor Microsoft Word and the spreadsheet Microsoft Excel, were created for the Macintosh.

But Gates was also working with IBM to develop a new operating system called OS/2. The two companies ran into numerous problems on this project. Some were technical, some arose from the fact that IBM laboratories were spread out across the country, leading to product turf wars, and some were a matter of developmental vision. Chris Peters, a Microsoft vice president, clarifies one of the main problems with OS/2 in *Microsoft Secrets*, a book on how the company develops its products, written with a great deal of input from Microsoft executives by Michael A. Cusmano and Richard W. Selby: "OS/2 was an attempt where they tried to change things . . . they tried to make things 10 percent better but completely different, and nobody wanted 10 percent better. We have a rule of thumb that things have to be twice as good before they can be different, if you're trying for consistency."

Gates became increasingly frustrated with the project, as did Nathan Myhrvold, the technical wizard who had joined Microsoft in 1986 when Gates bought his tiny company and hired its six-person staff. IBM, for its part, was annoyed with Gates's attitude, and by 1989, the two companies decided to call a halt to their collaboration following the release of the first OS/2 product. Microsoft had already released its first

The rate of change of technology is faster today than ever before. Some of the big advances of the past, several generations would go by as it became popular—the telephone, even the TV set. Within the space of a single generation we'll go from computers being something you can ignore very easily to the point where in most jobs, and to really be in touch, you'll have to be comfortable with using it as a tool.

—BILL GATES, 1995

two Windows operating systems, in 1985 and 1987, but they had been commercial failures. The company then brought out Windows 3.0 in 1990, which overcame the 640K boundary of MS-DOS (a limitation in the amount of information that could be stored). Work was already under way on Windows 3.1, but Gates was taking an enormous risk, essentially "betting the company" on the eventual success of Windows 3.1. Without the IBM tie-in, Windows 3.1 had to be a major success. It was, becoming the standard for personal computers and swamping IBM's latest version of OS/2.

Even as Windows 3.1 was being released in 1992, the final papers in the IBM/Microsoft divorce were at last being signed. Microsoft retained the rights to the NT (for New Technology) software it had developed. (This was used for allowing networks of PCs to work together, and would become increasingly important in the years ahead. It would be incorporated into Windows 95, and its successors would be crucial to Microsoft's move into the corporate PC market in 1997.) IBM was given use of Windows code, but only until late 1993. And Microsoft was also given a royalty on OS/2 sales—which would prove to be small potatoes when Windows 3.1 took over the market. Microsoft did pay IBM a flat fee, reported to be in the neighborhood of $25 million, for the use of some IBM patents. But given the eventual success of Windows 3.1, it is clear in hindsight that Microsoft took IBM to the cleaners on this resolution of their partnership.

The popularity of Windows 3.1 can be measured by the fact that it was installed on seventy million personal computers that already had been bought worldwide at the time of its 1992 introduction, and on ninety percent of the new computers bought between then and the August 1995 introduction of Windows 95. In terms of personal computer software, Microsoft had not merely achieved dominance, it had over-

Microsoft does the great majority of its software development in the United States, but that could change in the future. Our motive would not be to save money, however. We create software for the world and our success depends on drawing on a world of talent.

—BILL GATES, 1996

whelmed the competition. From 1992, Bill Gates was on a steady climb, not just year by year, or month by month, but week by week, toward becoming the world's richest man.

Developing the successor to Windows 3.1 proved to be arduous. For one thing, it moved from 16-bit processing to 32-bit processing, made possible by the increasing speed and capacity of Intel's Pentium chips. This was a new ball game, which made it feasible to introduce a wide range of new features but greatly complicated the writing of code and also increased the number of bugs in the system. In addition, Windows 95 was delayed by Microsoft's belated recognition of the importance of the Internet.

Windows 95 took off "like a bat out of hell," to use an old phrase that sums up the attitude of Microsoft's competitors. Between its August 24, 1995 release date and the end of the fiscal quarter on September 30, 1995, it sold an estimated seven million copies. This was a much higher number than either the computer industry or Wall Street analysts had expected. Microsoft itself had announced that it expected to sell thirty million copies in the first year; at this rate, it would reach that number in less than five months. There had been enormous media coverage of the Windows 95 launch, and from now on, Bill Gates, who had hardly been ignored in the past, would become one of the most heavily profiled and interviewed men on earth, commanding almost as many magazine covers as movie and music stars.

But he was hardly resting on his laurels. His book, *The Road Ahead*, surged immediately to the top of the best-seller lists at the end of 1995. The book contained a bound-in envelope containing a CD-ROM, which included, to quote the jacket description, "the complete book text with hundreds of multimedia hyperlinks, a special interview with Bill Gates, video demonstrations of future technology, a

Television shows will continue to be broadcast as they are today for synchronous consumption— at the same time they are first broadcast. After they air, these shows—as well as thousands of movies and virtually all other kinds of video—will be available whenever you want to view them. You'll be able to watch the new episode of *Seinfeld* at 9:00 P.M. on Thursday night, or at 9:18 P.M., or at 11:00 A.M. on Saturday. If you don't care for his brand of humor, there will be thousands of other choices.

—BILL GATES, 1995

World Wide Web browser and more." The book was co-written with Nathan Myhrvold, Microsoft group vice president, Applications & Content Group, and the Pulitzer Prize–winning journalist Peter Rinearson. Gates's own profits from the book were used to fund "a grant for technology in education administration through the National Foundation for Improvement in Education."

In 1996, Microsoft joined with NBC to create MSNBC, linking the Microsoft Web Network with a broadcast cable television entity. In 1996 and 1997 Microsoft also acquired or made significant investments in company after company that offered possible keys to the development of the coming information highway, including makers of set-top boxes that would allow the integration of television and the Internet, and of audio systems linking PCs and the Internet. These investments were proceeding at such a pace that by the summer of 1997, a few Wall Street analysts began suggesting that if Microsoft had any weakness it was the possibility that it might be spreading itself too thin. Bill Gates did not see it that way, of course. He had pointed out again and again that the information highway was still in the formative stage, and that there were several different directions in which it could go. Indeed, most analysts looked on his acquisitions and investments as a wise policy, protecting Microsoft's interests on several fronts and thus making it a player no matter what happened. As Microsoft edged closer to the entertainment world with MSNBC and various technical investments that had potential entertainment linkages, Gates had to put down rumors and questions about the possibility of his going so far as to buy a movie studio. Perhaps noting the problems that Sony had run into with its acquisition of Columbia Pictures, Gates squelched any such idea.

But if Gates was showing increasing interest in the en-

Computers aren't easy enough to use. They're not inexpensive enough to maintain. They're not effective enough at gathering certain kinds of information. The competition to solve these problems is fierce, but even without competition the challenge of making far better products would be very stimulating.

—BILL GATES, 1996

tertainment aspects of the emerging information highway, he was also moving aggressively on the computer software front. In mid-1997 he garnered several magazine cover stories on his major push into the networked business computer market. The May 1997 *Fortune* had a huge, grainy close-up of the center of Bill Gates's bespectacled face, with a slight grin that could easily be read as rapacious, featuring the headline "Gates' Greatest Power Grab (It's Working)." Gates believes that Microsoft's Windows NT will, combined with its BackOffice software package, eventually displace the UNIX system as the preferred choice for corporate computer networking. UNIX servers, the chief product of Sun Microsystems, have been the backbone of corporate computer systems, running as many as sixty-four processors simultaneously. The current Windows NT can run only eight computers at once, far too few for such things as hotel and airline reservation systems. But Microsoft's initial aim is to capture the small business market, and it is selling Windows NT for what *Fortune* calls a "cutthroat $625." Microsoft has as much as $1 billion in advanced research currently under way, the vast majority of it devoted to increasing the number of processors Windows NT can run. And for smaller companies, the Windows NT/BackOffice combination has already displaced UNIX. The chip manufacturer Intel, which has worked closely with Microsoft on many projects, as well as most of the PC manufacturers, see an enormously profitable future in the development of NT software. The overall business market is estimated at nearly $60 billion. Thus, if Microsoft succeeds in the business PC world in any measure that even approaches its domination of the individual PC market, Microsoft stands to become not just a behemoth but an unstoppable juggernaut.

Over the years, competitors and some PC users have

Name a Microsoft product that's successful and isn't a top-rated product. We don't have one.

—BILL GATES, on the quality of Microsoft products, 1994

suggested that Microsoft's enormous success has been a marketing one rather than a technical one. The claim is made that there have been better software products produced by other companies, but that Microsoft's "steamroller" sales tactics have squashed such superior alternatives flat. These complaints overlook two important facts. The first is that when users or software reviewers in specialized or general interest publications take note of deficiencies in Microsoft products, the problems get fixed, sometimes right away, sometimes in the next upgrade of the product. In addition, as Bill Gates likes to note, his company's products have won numerous prestigious awards. As far back as 1983, Microsoft's Multiplan application for Apple II was chosen by *InfoWorld* as the software program of the year. Such awards have come regularly over the years, but 1994 was a particularly triumphant one. Its Office 4.0 and Windows NT 3.5 won the annual *PC Magazine* awards for technical excellence in the categories of applications and systems software, while Word was named best word-processing product, and Access—an entry-level database management program for individual users—was cited as best database product. Access, it is important to note, was originally purchased by Microsoft; it is sold both separately and as a part of Office. That hardly serves as an example of squashing the competition—Microsoft saw a good product and acquired it to make its own product better. Some will inevitably charge that such acquisitions are power grabs, but millions of customers are more likely to feel gratitude that the Access database is part of the most popular office suite on the market.

CHAPTER FOUR

RUNNING MICROSOFT

No one company can single-handedly make digital devices viable . . . cable television and telephone companies face the challenge of building the required digital infrastructure. Content companies must author their information in interesting and enticing ways. Traditional PC application software developers have to create the basic motivating applications and tools for the creative and content communities. And systems software companies must develop the underlying software that links these devices to each other and to the vast array of personal computers that are already an established element of the digital infrastructure.

—BILL GATES, 1992

The phrase *corporate campus* can be applied to the head-quarters of many major businesses around the world, at least in terms of their layout and general appearance. They are a further refinement of the "industrial parks" that began appearing in the 1970s, low-lying buildings scattered across considerable tracts of suburban land, separated by carefully tended swards of grass and shaded by clumps of trees. The original industrial parks were usually home to several businesses, deliberately designed to meld with the nearby residential suburbs, and standing in sharp contrast to the central city office towers that so many corporations were leaving behind.

But the corporate campus, home to a single company, has become particularly associated with high-technology firms, especially those in the computer field. These parklike headquarters do resemble the campuses of many small colleges and seem in tune with the laid-back, informally dressed image of the young technical wizards who inhabit them. But for all the tossing of Frisbees between the trees, and the rec rooms and gyms that are available for use, corporate campuses are home to some of the most prodigiously dedicated workers in the world. At computer companies like Apple and Microsoft, the serene, almost bucolic appearance of the workplace masks the extraordinarily intense, stressful work being done. When a major new product is in development—which is most of the time—employees are expected to put in working hours that early-twentieth-century reformers and union leaders would look upon with horror. In the final months before a crucial and much-ballyhooed product like Windows 95 is launched, many programmers may be found sleeping on office couches at the end of eighteen-hour workdays, not even bothering to go home. Of course, these people, unlike the workers of

Passionate leadership won't succeed if contradictory signals are sent. If you pump up your sales force at a meeting and tell them, "The most important goal is to make customers happy," you can't go back the next day and say, "Your quota just got doubled, so get out there ands sell twice as much."

—BILL GATES, 1996

the industrial revolution, are often able to purchase stock in the company they work for, and love what they are doing for a living.

The Microsoft corporate campus covers two hundred and seventy acres—it is constantly referred to as "sprawling"—in Redmond, Washington, a suburb of Seattle. Its scattered buildings of different sizes mean that small groups can work off in a far corner of the campus, or several groups can be brought together in a larger building when the need arises. There is a clear intent to play down the idea that working in any particular building carries greater status, but, from all reports, there is inevitably a special aura around Building 8, where Gates has his own office. However, in keeping with a company where corporate jockeying is discouraged by having numerous people hold the same title, Gates's office is far from the luxurious showplace favored by many CEOs. According to *Time*, the furniture is "standard-issue" and the decorative touches are minimal, dominated by an enormous photo of a Pentium chip. As might be expected, there are photographs of Leonardo da Vinci and Einstein, as well as one of Henry Ford. That one is of special interest. By Gates's own testimony it is there not so much to remind him of Ford's famous goal of seeing to it that every American family owned a car—a goal that Gates and others have proclaimed for the personal computer—but to remind him of the fact that Ford's stubbornness and lack of vision on several fronts eventually allowed many competitors to steal a march on him.

Gates is profoundly aware of the conventional wisdom that the leader in any great leap forward in technology will fail to see the next one coming. "Success is a lousy teacher," he wrote at the beginning of the third chapter of

Bill brings to the company the idea that conflict can be a good thing. The difference from P&G (Procter & Gamble) is striking. Politeness was at a premium there. Bill knows it's important to avoid that gentle civility that keeps you from getting to the heart of an issue quickly. He likes it when anyone, even a junior employee, challenges him, and you know he respects you when he starts shouting back.

—STEVE BALLMER, *Time*, 1997

The Road Ahead, titled "Lessons from the Computer Industry." "It seduces smart people into thinking they can't lose." In that chapter he goes on to discuss the failure of first- and second-wave computer giants like IBM, Digital Equipment Corporation, and Wang Laboratories to see the coming personal computer revolution. Gates not only saw it coming while he was still a teenager but he also understood the crucial role that software would play in that revolution. His worst fear seems to be that someday someone will be writing about him as he does about Ken Olsen and An Wang—as a man who missed the next great development. In several speeches and interviews over the years, Gates has spoken of "running scared" or being "scared all the time," in terms of staying ahead of the game. In recent years, however, he has downplayed those earlier remarks, apparently feeling that the word "scared" is a little too colloquial and adolescent; he has taken instead to talking about meeting new challenges and emphasizing the "fun" he still derives from beating competitors to the punch.

Nevertheless, the way Microsoft runs is clearly designed to avoid the possibility of missing the next big turn in that road ahead. It starts with the people Microsoft hires. The phrase that keeps popping up in respect to the kind of employee the company favors is *intellectual bandwidth.* According to many observers, the company looks for IQ, an open and inquiring mind, and a gift for ingenious problem solving more than for already acquired knowledge. In some ways this goes against the grain of the stereotypical image of the narrowly focused "computer nerd." The Microsoft philosophy appears to reflect the idea that it is easier to train a brilliant mind to do new kinds of work than it is to train someone with great technical knowledge to think creatively. This doesn't mean that already acquired

Sometimes I envy the people who still get to program. After I stopped programming for Microsoft, I used to say half-jokingly in meetings, "Maybe I'll come in this weekend and write it myself." I don't say that any more, but I think about it.

—BILL GATES, 1995

knowledge is disparaged, but rather that the person who has it must also demonstrate an ability to seek new knowledge.

Some say flatly that the company looks for "Bill clones." Indeed, several journalists who have been allowed to sit in on the meetings that Bill Gates constantly holds with project groups have reported that his programmers often rock back and forth when they are thinking, just as Gates does. They also note, however, that these meetings are very democratic, and that those present are encouraged to challenge and debate statements made by their boss. To have him yell "That's the stupidest thing I've ever heard"—which he often does—is taken not as a rebuke but as a badge of honor. The vast majority of the young programmers are male, although there are numerous women who work in other areas.

It is central to the way Microsoft is run that Bill Gates is himself a programmer of genius. Nathan Myhrvold, the head of Microsoft's advanced research division and a man of great intellectual breadth, told *Time,* "There are two types of tech companies, those where the guy in charge knows how to surf, and those where he depends on experts on the beach to guide him." Gates is a preeminent example of the guy who knows how to surf. That means that the average of three meetings a day he holds with project groups can be run with great dispatch. No time need be wasted on explaining what even the most technical matter involves, and that in turn cuts down on the necessity to "schmooze," which the other kind of CEO often must do to create loyalty and respect. Office politics are not one of Bill Gates's interests.

One particular aspect of office politics that Gates particularly dislikes is the shifting of blame. He has made it clear

There used to be a sofa in Microsoft's telephone customer support service called "the Mail-Merge couch"—named for a feature in our word-processing program that lets users customize form letters. The early version of Mail Merge was so complicated that whenever a customer called for help, our representative would lie down on the couch to take the call, knowing the conversation was likely to last a long time. Clearly something was wrong.

—BILL GATES, 1996

in several articles and speeches that he has tried to avoid that kind of situation at Microsoft. Mistakes are to be learned from, he insists, and instead of wasting time and energy on assigning blame, he wants the focus to be on fixing the problem. In one of his newspaper columns, Gates tells about the discovery of a bug in the Macintosh spreadsheet software called Multiplan, developed by Microsoft and released in 1983. The Multiplan team asked if a free corrected version should be sent out to those who had already purchased Multiplan. Even though that was twenty thousand customers, Gates immediately said yes. From his point of view there was no discussion necessary, even though it cost $250,000 to ship the corrected version.

Gates went on to point out that he had made his own mistake on the original 1981 version of Multiplan, taking out some features so that it could run on the Apple II, as well as on the higher-powered IBM PC. That opened the way for a new company, Lotus, to bring out its own superior spreadsheet, and Lotus 1–2–3 knocked the original Multiplan flat. Everyone, Gates believes, makes mistakes sometimes, often expensive ones, and it is particularly easy to make such an error in an industry that is constantly exploring new areas. So he sees no point in the blame game.

On the other side of the coin, Gates does sometimes worry about the fact that Microsoft has had so few real failures that it may encounter problems dealing with them when they do occur. For that reason, he notes, he hired Craig Mundie in 1992. Mundie knew all about failure. He had been a cofounder of a supercomputer business named Alliant Computer Systems, which had gone under as the market had changed. Gates notes that "Mundie under-

Frankly, one of the challenges facing Microsoft is that many of its employees have not suffered much failure yet. Quite a few have never been involved with a project that didn't succeed. As a result, success may be taken for granted, which is dangerous. With this in mind, we have deliberately recruited a few managers with experience in failing companies.

—BILL GATES, 1995

stands his mistakes and drew keen lessons from them," becoming a particularly able asset to Microsoft.

Microsoft now has more than twenty thousand employees, including a modest number overseas. In 1992 alone, it hired twenty-five hundred people. This is a far cry from the early days, when Gates initially balked at Steve Ballmer's insistence on hiring an additional fifty employees on top of the thirty-five that then worked for the company. But with $9 billion in cash on hand, Gates doesn't have to worry about becoming overextended in the way he once did, and by comparison with many companies, Microsoft is a fairly lean organization. It does have offices in a number of foreign countries, and parcels out certain work to foreign technical people. In the summer of 1997, the company also announced a million-dollar joint venture in advanced research with Cambridge University in England, a center of scientific thought for centuries, where the celebrated physicist Stephen Hawking, whose son works for Microsoft in Redmond, holds the same university chair that originally was created for Sir Isaac Newton.

But while Gates has been willing to greatly expand his workforce, he has assiduously avoided the IBM model of having many different research centers scattered across America. He has stated that when Microsoft was working directly with IBM, he was struck by the "wasteful inter-site rivalry" and "pointless contention" between the various IBM laboratories. A closer association with Hewlett-Packard in recent years has somewhat lessened Gates's concern about the multi-site model, however. He says that Hewlett-Packard, by giving a particular lab a set agenda that does not change and then enlarging or shrinking that lab on the basis of its success, is able to keep that kind of rivalry under control. It has been suggested that the Hewlett-Pack-

Our top executives have an annual retreat, a tradition that began when my company had only twenty employees. These retreats have proved invaluable over the years. For instance, during the days of Microsoft's partnership with IBM, one of the small breakout groups would always examine the question, How should we prepare ourselves in case our most important partner decides not to work with us any more? Having gone through that exercise over a period of five years, we were more prepared to cope when IBM pulled out of the partnership in 1992.

—BILL GATES, 1996

ard example lies behind Gates's willingness to enter into the Cambridge University venture, but at least for now Gates has no plans to open other Microsoft sites in the United States.

Microsoft employees are fairly well paid. More important, however, is the fact that they can acquire stock options in the company. It has been estimated that more than twenty-five hundred present and former Microsoft employees are now millionaires due to exercising their stock options. But employees of the company are kept on their toes by regular reorganizations, which have taken place about every two years from the beginning. Gates views reorganizations as vital to keeping his company's employees creative, challenged, and efficient. He sees them as a way to renew people's intellectual juices. He particularly likes the idea of moving people back and forth between product development and customer-related jobs, if the individuals have capabilities in both areas, because it helps to "conceive and deliver better products" in a customer-driven industry. While he recognizes the risk of having both jobs less well executed, and of losing some managers who aren't happy with a new position or aren't right for it, he feels such drawbacks to reorganization are acceptable, within limits. To lose too many people or have too many jobs less well done is another matter—and one that Microsoft has been able to avoid, in part perhaps because computer technology continues to change and grow so rapidly that there is a built-in excitement to moving into a new area for most employees. Gates clearly does not want workers whose eyes are chiefly fixed on climbing a hierarchical ladder.

Despite the regular reorganizations and the flexibility Gates sought to sustain, Microsoft was becoming a much larger company, hiring thousands of new employees every

Reorganizations are expected around Microsoft. But that doesn't mean they don't create anxiety. They do, for almost everyone affected—including me. My concern is whether or not we're making the right decisions, and whether key employees will be enthusiastic about their new roles. I gain confidence about a potential reorganization when I see that it makes clear what every group is supposed to do, minimizes the dependencies and overlap between groups, and offers developing employees larger responsibilities.

—BILL GATES, 1996

year in the early 1990s. Big companies, as Gates was all too well aware, can get complacent, flabby, or unwieldy very easily. Trying to stay ahead of the game, Microsoft was developing new products in many different areas. The most important project in the first half of the 1990s was Windows 95, originally code-named Chicago. This operating system was designed not just to preserve Microsoft's domination of the market for personal computer operating systems but also to blow its competitors out of the water. The next research and development priority was the so-called information highway, which had been a red-hot media topic since the 1992 election, when Al Gore had started pushing it. This gateway to the communications future was to be based on interactive television (including a putative choice of five hundred channels) controlled through a box on the top of television sets. The race was on to develop both the hardware and software for this wave of the future. Media hype (driven in part by the fact that television itself was at the center of the projected highway) had driven up public expectations to a high pitch, with much loose talk about it becoming a reality in two or three years. Gates himself tried to tone down the hype, saying this revolution was further down the line than magazine cover stories suggested. He was fully aware that there were enormous technical problems to be overcome on the hardware end of things, and that it was impossible to develop software for nonexistent hardware.

Even so, Microsoft was working hard on the basic software, which could subsequently be adjusted to whatever hardware came into existence, as well as investing in and forging alliances with companies that were likely to play crucial roles in the eventual highway. And because of this concentration on the information highway, Microsoft was

Before we can enjoy the benefits of the applications and appliances, the information highway has to exist. It doesn't yet. This may surprise some people, who hear everything from a long-distance telephone network to the Internet described as "the information superhighway." The truth is that the full highway is unlikely to be available in homes for at least a decade.

—BILL GATES, 1995

slow on the uptake in realizing the importance of another communications revolution that was already happening—the Internet. The beginnings of the Internet went back as far as 1969, when the U.S. Department of Defense set about designing a computer network that would not be put out of business by a nuclear attack. Instead of having government computers linked to a central point, the new system, created by ARPANET (Advanced Research Project Agency), made it possible for individual computers to communicate directly with one another. That way, all surviving computers after an attack would still be in touch, even if they were widely scattered. The next step in broadening usage of what would become the Internet occurred when, as James Wallace describes in his 1997 book *Overdrive*, Tim Berners-Lee, a researcher at the European Laboratory for Particle Physics in Geneva, Switzerland, designed a new kind of document description language known as Hyper-Text Markup Language, or HTML. The language, which consisted of a set of codes that were added to a document, was a way to format a document to enable the embedding of graphics, sound clips, or other multimedia, and to link a document with any other document on any other computer on the Internet.

HTML became a favored way for scientists at laboratories around the world to exchange information, but it required scientists to make use of the complex UNIX code, which limited what became known as the World Wide Web to a relatively small number of users. The development of a simplified Internet "browser" was undertaken by a twenty-one-year-old software writer at the University of Illinois at Urbana-Champaign's National Center for Super-computing Applications. The young man's name was Marc Andreessen, who would go on to become one of the best

It has been clear for years that gigantic changes await societies once people can easily exchange large amounts of digital information across distances. Many of us have long expected that the combination of powerful but inexpensive PCs and drastically falling communications costs would eventually set off an explosive positive-feedback cycle, in which the growth in the number of users and in the amount of valuable content would feed each other. The same spiraling dynamic has driven the stunning growth of the computer industry.

—BILL GATES, 1996

known and most controversial of a new generation of "computer geniuses." Without telling their superiors, Andreessen and a friend named Eric Bina, along with a few others on the staff of the center, spent two months creating a browser they called Mosaic. It was then distributed free over the Internet, as HTML had been earlier. Suddenly, the World Wide Web was accessible to people who were not computer experts. It was the spring of 1993, and the entire world of computers was about to change.

Gates would later say that his first introduction to the Internet through a Mosaic browser took place in April of 1993. But he didn't pay all that much attention and, according to several sources, didn't take another look until October. At this point he was still focused, as were the media, on the information superhighway. He was concerned about the fledgling on-line services, Prodigy, CompuServ, and America Online, which were rapidly signing up subscribers to their offerings of various information services provided by magazines, newspapers, scientific journals, and multimedia companies like Time-Warner. The smallest of the three companies at the time, America Online, had been sounded out by Microsoft about being taken over and made a part of Windows 95, but the company's chairman, Steve Case, had ambitious plans and didn't want to sell. Gates thus gave the go-ahead for Microsoft to develop its own on-line service to be included in Windows 95, although he worried that there wasn't time to get it ready for the planned June 1994 release of Windows 95. That release date would ultimately be pushed back twice, first to December 1994, and finally to August of 1995.

Even as work got under way to develop a proprietary Microsoft on-line service (code-named Marvel, a fact that Marvel Comics got wind of and objected to), there were a

At Microsoft, we have hundreds of people whose job it is to create the software that will make the information highway an idea worth having. The way in which you find and interact with information will change. It's not going to change tomorrow . . . but when that day comes, we will be a major player in delivering the software that makes it go.

—Bill Gates, 1993

few people at Microsoft who believed that it was vital to recognize the broader potential of the Internet, and to capitalize on it as quickly as possible. One of the strongest believers in the explosive nature of the Internet was Ron Glaser, who was actually on leave after ten years at Microsoft and in the process of planning his own company. But Bill Gates persuaded him to come in as a consultant to the Marvel project for perhaps a dozen hours a week. As James Wallace reports in *Overdrive*, Glaser recruited Russ Siegelman, who lobbied for the Marvel project and was put in charge of it.

It was Glaser's intention to push for a nonproprietary Internet site with Siegelman, but shortly before the two were scheduled to meet, Siegelman had a brain aneurysm that required an operation. He would be sidelined until December 1993. Glaser is quoted by Wallace as saying, "I did not want to randomize the team while Russ was out getting well. So I decided to basically teach his staff Internet 101." But the lesson didn't take, and Glaser didn't want to go directly to Gates on the matter while Siegelman was out. He did give his "Internet 101" material to Gates's technical assistant, Steve Sinofsky, and he and two senior programmers, James Allard and Ben Slivka, would ultimately play crucial roles in getting Microsoft into full-scale Internet involvement.

Although Bill Gates was given a major demonstration of what was taking place on the Internet by Steve Sinofsky, it would take the arrival of Netscape's Mosaic Navigator in October of 1994 to fully galvanize the vast resources of Microsoft behind the creation of a major Internet presence. Netscape was a tiny company, formed by Jim Clark, the former head of Silicon Graphics (the *Jurassic Park* computer effects company), from which he had resigned in February

The surging popularity of the communications network called the Internet is the most important single development in the computer industry since the IBM PC was introduced in 1981. . . . Like the PC, the Internet is a tidal wave. It will wash over the computer industry and many others, drowning those who don't learn to swim in its waves.

—BILL GATES, 1995

of 1994 following differences with other executives over the company's direction, and Marc Andreessen, the whiz kid who had been the principal developer of Mosaic at the Urbana-Champaign campus of the University of Illinois. Andreessen had just graduated, in December of 1993, with a bachelor's degree in computer science. Clark tracked him down and sent him an e-mail. The two of them then persuaded Andreessen's friend Eric Bina, as well as a number of others who had worked on the first Mosaic project, to join the company. The company was formed in early April of 1994, and had its first version of its new browser ready just six months later.

As James Wallace recounts, "By the fall of 1994, when thousands of computer users began downloading Netscape's new browser, the number of people using the Internet was exploding by about ten percent a month. Many of these new users were interested in just one area of the Internet—the World Wide Web. From some fifty commercial sites in January 1993, by October the Web had about ten thousand." Microsoft had had a small browser development team in place since August, and was talking to two companies, Booklink Technologies and Spyglass, about the possibility of licensing their browsers. Spyglass had the rights, ironically, to the original Mosaic developed at the University of Illinois by Marc Andreessen and his cohorts, while Booklink had developed its own system. To make maters more complicated, Netscape had just taken this new name in the fall of 1994. It had originally been called Mosaic Communications, a name to which the University of Illinois violently objected. In addition to changing the name of the company to Netscape Communications Corporation, Clark and Andreessen had had to pay $2.7 million in damages,

Most media today is financed through advertising, and I expect the Internet to follow this same pattern. But interactivity is an advantage that Net advertising will have over the traditional kind. The initial message will need only to attract attention. Users will be able to click on ads to get additional information, and advertisers will be able to measure how often viewers are doing so. Accurate measurement of advertising's effectiveness has been a long time coming, and the Internet will finally provide it.

—BILL GATES, 1996

which was split between the university and Spyglass, according to James Wallace.

Microsoft came close to making a deal with Booklink for its browser, but the tough terms caused Booklink to switch at the last moment to an offer from America Online. Microsoft now was placed in a difficult position. It was clear that in order to have a browser as part of Windows 95 (already twice delayed) for its August 1995 release, it would have to license a browser and incorporate it in a somewhat changed form into Windows 95 instead of developing one from scratch. Bill Gates finally signed the contract with Spyglass on December 16, 1994.

By the time Windows 95 came out in August of 1995, Netscape was sufficiently well established that it has been able to remain a major player in the browser market. But by turning his company around in a single year to take advantage of the Internet phenomenon, Bill Gates was able to see to it that his company did not miss out entirely on this important turn in the road. Gates himself has become one of the foremost promoters of the Internet, more than making up for his initial lack of focus with a broad vision of the Internet's place in the future development of computer technology. Indeed, in a step that nicely completed the circle, Microsoft made a sizable but undisclosed investment in July 1997 in another Seattle area company, Progressive Networks. The company specializes in enabling software for Web-based audio presentations and very low-speed video. The company was founded by and is headed by none other than Ron Glaser, the former Microsoft executive who worked so diligently to make Microsoft executives fully aware of the importance of the Internet.

CHAPTER FIVE

TOUGH COMPETITION

Just because somebody with a calculator recently deemed me the richest businessman in the world doesn't mean that I'm a genius. My success in business has largely been the result of my ability to focus on long-term goals and ignore short-term distractions. Taking a long-term view doesn't require brilliance, but it does require dedication.

—BILL GATES, 1995

No one in the business world can become as successful and as powerful as Bill Gates has without acquiring enemies. And Gates has many enemies. Few of them seem to care all that much about his enormous wealth; most of them have made fortunes themselves and have, like Gates, started giving money away. They do not begrudge Gates his success in the usual envious terms, either. What makes some of them very angry is that they believe Microsoft, because of its market dominance in operating software, which began with MS-DOS and became even greater with the Windows series, is able to squeeze companies with better systems into a marginal position and put them out of business entirely. It is, ultimately, the power to do that which creates the anger.

It is hardly surprising when competitors in any field of business bad-mouth one another's products. The kind of negative attack ads that have become so common in politics aren't allowed in industry, by law, but there are subtle ways for a crack advertising company to make invidious comparisons (for example, we see them all the time in the "cola wars"). But there's nothing to prevent one chief executive from running down another company's products in interviews with the press. And if a company gets angry enough, and its lawyers think a case can be made, complaints can be filed with the Federal Trade Commission. That's what began to happen in the computer world in the early 1990s. There were a number of competitors making complaints about Microsoft's business practices, but the two best known are Phillipe Kahn, the French-born founder of Borland International, and Raymond Noorda of Novell Data Systems.

Kahn was already thirty when he arrived in California in 1982. He was late getting into the computer field, but

Microsoft Word, which is our word processor, is used to write eighty percent of all the documents that are created in the world today, because it's available in Chinese, and German, and every language you can name, but in no sense does providing that tool give us any influence over what people choose to write.

—BILL GATES, downplaying the power of Microsoft, 1995

he had been trained as a mathematician, and his technical wizardry soon made the tiny company he founded over an auto repair shop in Scott's Valley near San Jose into the third biggest software company behind Microsoft and Novell. Within a year he had introduced an inexpensive computer programming language called Turbo Pascal. As the *New York Times* reported, "He sold his programming language mail order at a fraction of the price charged by larger rivals like IBM and Digital Research." He followed that with Sidekick, which would become the most popular scheduling and information manager software for personal computers.

Despite the respect Kahn had as a technical genius, he also had a reputation as a wild character. He even styled himself as a "barbarian," drove cars at speeds that brought him endless tickets, spent a lot of time sailing yachts, and played the saxophone, recording two albums with well-known jazz professionals—paid for by his company. He and Gates loathed one another. Kahn said that Microsoft was run like "Nazi Germany," and Gates told *Time*, "Phillipe Kahn is good at playing the saxophone and sailing, but he's not good at making money." According to James Wallace in *Overdrive*, one group at Microsoft had T-shirts made up that read "Delete Phillipe." And that's exactly what Gates set about doing, by buying one of Borland's chief rivals for database products, Fox Software. The deal went through in early 1992 for one hundred seventy-three million dollars; Microsoft used its sales force to push its FoxPro from ten percent to fifteen percent of the market in a few months. In December of that year, Microsoft introduced its own database product, Access, and sold it at a steep discount to undercut Borland. Borland began posting losses, and Kahn had to keep reducing the number of the

Software companies are sometimes criticized for designing software that works best on the newest, most powerful machines. But it almost has to be that way because advances in computer hardware let software companies make products that are easier to use relative to what they accomplish.

—BILL GATES, 1995

company's employees as he made mistakes of his own and fell behind in delivering new products. The personal animosity Khan felt toward Gates was hardly eased when his former wife started dating the Microsoft founder.

The antipathy between Raymond Noorda and Gates was more straightforward, growing out of tough Microsoft business stances. Noorda was not a technical person, but he was a frugal manager, and had turned around a struggling Novell when he was brought in to run it in 1982, at the age of fifty-eight. Gates had managed to block Novell's attempt to purchase another software company, Aston-Tate, in 1988 (Aston-Tate was later bought by Borland International, in a disastrous deal that ran up Borland's debt). Still, Noorda had been willing to talk when Gates had approached him about a possible merger between the two companies in 1991. Novell was the top dog in the business of producing networking software to link computers to one another, an area that was a real weakness for Microsoft, but one that Gates had great interest in and would continue to move forward on. But the deal with Novell was called off by Microsoft, and Noorda came away from the experience convinced that Gates had only been interested in getting a look at Novell's inside workings and information.

Kahn and Noorda were thus both delighted to assist the Federal Trade Commission in its investigation of Microsoft's business practices during the first half of the 1990s. The FTC's interest had originally been aroused by the IBM/Microsoft agreement to develop OS/2 together, which immediately got antitrust noses twitching. When that agreement ultimately fell apart, the FTC had so much information on Microsoft and had received so many complaints about the way it operated from competitors that it kept right on investigating. Antitrust cases are always extremely

Given the amount of mud people have thrown up on the wall to see if it sticks, I think it's pretty amazing that not a speck of dirt has ever stuck.

—BILL GATES, on competitors' charges that Microsoft is ruthless, 1993

complex, and, in a new field like computers, the law is often only vaguely applicable. But there were two main areas that the FTC was looking at. The first had to do with Microsoft's agreements with the computer manufacturers, which gave them large discounts on the use of Microsoft DOS, provided a royalty was paid to Microsoft on every computer, regardless of whether it had DOS installed on it. Why, the question was asked, would a PC maker ever install an operating system from a competitor when it was already paying for DOS? The second main area of concern stemmed from complaints from competitors that, contrary to regulations, they did not receive the information they needed from Microsoft on new operating systems in a timely fashion that would allow them to develop their own applications systems that work with, for example, DOS for Windows. There was a suspicion that the Microsoft applications division was getting such information first, giving it a head start, despite the fact that regulations required competitors to receive it at the same time.

Raymond Noorda was leading the charge against Microsoft, with as many as seven lawyers active in the case, but Borland and several other companies also tried to sway the FTC commissioners to take action against Microsoft. Although the general public was largely unaware of what was going on—FTC investigations are far too complicated for the sound-bite reporting of the evening news programs, and get reported only when a case comes to a head—the *Wall Street Journal* and the business pages of other leading newspapers followed the case closely. James Wallace gives a lengthy after-the-fact treatment of the matter in *Overdrive*, but it became a story with an anticlimactic ending. On February 5, 1993, the five FTC commissioners met to take a vote on whether action should be taken against Microsoft,

It's fine for the antitrust authorities to look into what is a very important industry and say, you know, "What are the dynamics here?" As they look at it, what they're going to find is that we're all just, you know, fighting to get our message across and get these new products out as fast as we can. And it's exactly what government should look to in a market—U.S. companies doing very, very well and not being at all complacent.

—BILL GATES, to Charlie Rose, 1996

and with one commissioner recusing himself because of a conflict of interest, the remaining four split evenly. The matter was taken up again, after further study, on July 21, 1993, with the same result. The Justice Department's Antitrust Division then took the unusual step of getting involved.

The Justice Department case, led by Anne Bingaman, who had been appointed head of the Antitrust Division by President Clinton, went on for another year, and was finally settled with a consent agreement approved by Bill Gates. It essentially changed the kind of licensing agreement Microsoft could demand from computer makers; from now on they could send out computers that had other companies' operating systems without still having to pay a fee to Microsoft. This was claimed to "level the playing field," but the press took the view that Gates had just been given a slap on the wrist.

All consent decrees have to be approved by a federal judge, who is assigned cases by lottery. The judge in this case was Stanley Sporkin, who also thought the consent decree was a slap on the wrist, and threw it out on February 14, 1994, infuriating not only Bill Gates but also Anne Bingaman. On appeal, with Microsoft and the Justice Department now on the same side, Sporkin's decision was overturned by a three-judge appeals panel, and Sporkin was chastised for having overstepped his authority. The case came to an end three days before the launch of Windows 95 on August 24, 1995.

Not only was Bill Gates temporarily free of government interference and about to present the world with what would become the most successful computer software ever devised, but the two men who had been his greatest enemies were gone from Borland and Novell. Phillipe Kahn

Scott hates PCs and he hates the fact that customers like PCs. When PCs were selling six million units a year he said that it was a stupid idea. Now PCs are selling seventy million units a year, and Scott's trying to tell corporations that they should just rip PCs away, that flexibility and empowerment is bad stuff. If he's using my image as part of that attack, then fine.

—BILL GATES, returning the compliments of
Sun CEO Scott McNealy, 1996

resigned—or was forced to resign by the board of directors—as head of the company he had founded a dozen years earlier, leaving on January 11, 1995. Kahn even showed up at the Windows 95 launch celebration; he had started a new company and needed to mend fences with Microsoft. As for Raymond Noorda, he had been gone from Novell for a year, retiring at the age of seventy, his memory failing.

Of course there were still plenty of competitors who disliked Bill Gates and regarded Microsoft as a dangerous gorilla of a company. The three who came to the fore to challenge Gates most openly were Jim Barksdale, the new CEO of Netscape, Scott McNealy of Sun Microsystems, and Larry Ellison of Oracle Systems Corporation. Barksdale is the most diplomatic of these competitors, and he can afford to be—Netscape beat Microsoft to the punch with an Internet browser, which still outsells Microsoft's version more than two to one. Ellison had said that "everybody hates Microsoft," but that is clearly wishful thinking. Scott McNealy is the most outspoken. He told *Newsweek,* "There's two camps, those in Redmond, who live on the Death Star, and the rest of us, the rebel forces." This is what McNealy told *Newsweek* in May of 1997. Of course, back in December of 1995, he had agreed to license Java—a computer language developed by his company that would become the standard for creating visual and audio effects on Internet web pages—to Microsoft. That was just good business. It would help establish Java as the standard, bring in plenty of cash, and prevent Microsoft from developing a rival language.

While such agreements between rivals—even personal enemies—occur in other fields, they are particularly common in the computer business, for several reasons. It has

But don't conclude that computer processing speed is out just because I don't use the very fastest personal computer available. Keep in mind that by many measures a 480 notebook computer like mine outperforms an IBM mainframe computer of twenty years ago—and costs perhaps one-five thousandth as much.

—BILL GATES, 1995

been fifty years since ENIAC's components could fill an entire railroad boxcar. Thanks to the microchip, computers in that time have become small enough so that a machine that can be held in one hand can do more calculations more quickly than ENIAC could. Yet, as anyone in the field will tell you, computers are still in their infancy. Thus computer businesses, whether they produce hardware, software, or both, have a vested interest in the kind of cross-fertilization that creates further new developments. The vast possibilities that still lie in the future certainly create intense competition, but they also require that competitors quite often cooperate with one another in order to move the entire industry to a higher level. It is doubtful, in fact, if there has ever been another field in which the phrase "good for the industry" has been used so often.

Microsoft itself, in spite of a dominance that drives both competitors and the government to worry about monopolistic practices, has created opportunities for dozens of other companies to develop specialized applications for its own products. Just as Microsoft was given an enormous push forward by its association with the then dominant IBM in the 1980s, so many smaller companies in the 1990s have been able to prosper, or indeed have come into being, because of the standards Microsoft has set. Rivals may launch lawsuits or push the government to take antitrust action, but they may also suddenly find themselves cooperating with Microsoft because it makes good business sense for everybody.

Again and again Bill Gates has defended his company's practices, sometimes testily, sometimes in lofty terms. When asked by *Time* whether Microsoft was trying to create a monopoly by embedding its Internet browser into Windows, he replied, "Any operating system without a

When you're lucky and successful, it's important not to get complacent. Luck can turn sour, and customers demand a lot from the people and companies they make successful. Big mistakes are rarely tolerated. I hope to remain successful, but there are no guarantees.

—BILL GATES, 1997

browser is going to be f——— out of business. Should we improve our product or go out of business." In softer terms, he told Charlie Rose, "Well, what Microsoft does is we ship software products and we keep trying to improve them. And so in that sense, yes, we are relentless. We're always hiring smart people. When you ship a great software product, there's nothing tough about it. There's nothing mean about it. People take it, put it in their computer and they decide if they like it and it's word of mouth that drives that."

It is also important to recognize that saying bad things about Bill Gates does not mean that he'll never work with you again. Ron Glaser, the former Microsoft executive who was instrumental, as a subsequent part-time consultant, in pushing Gates to recognize the importance of the Internet in 1994, said of his former boss in January of 1997, "He's Darwinian. He doesn't look for win-win situations with others, but for ways to make others lose. Success is defined as flattening the competition, not creating excellence." While Glaser also said he admired Gates's vision, such remarks might be expected to cause Gates to seek retribution, right? Wrong. Seven months later, Microsoft announced a significant but undisclosed investment in Glaser's own company, which specializes in computer sound systems. Gates may get angry, and he sometimes says harsh things about people who attack him, but he doesn't hold the kind of grudge that prevents him from making a subsequent deal if he sees it as good for Microsoft.

As stated before, Gates sometimes had a combative relationship with Microsoft cofounder Paul Allen, and Allen can still be critical at times, but that does not interfere with their friendship of a quarter century. Gates is a combative person. It's worth recalling that when he was sent to a

Well, I think, throughout our history, we wake up every day knowing that in the business of technology you have to think about what you are missing. What is the research or customer feedback that you should be paying more attention to? And how do you keep that pace of innovation very, very high? How do you make sure that you are hiring the very best people? And that kind of focus has helped drive us forward through all the milestones the company has had.

—BILL GATES, to Charlie Rose, 1996

psychologist as a teenager, the therapist ended up telling his mother that she would never win a battle with him and had to take another approach. In the long run, Gates became extremely close to her. It should also be kept in mind that when Gates shouts "That's the stupidest thing I ever heard" in meetings with his employees, it is taken as a badge of honor. It means Bill Gates is paying attention. That kind of person may sometimes be difficult to deal with, but the business world is full of people who just smile at you and then stab you in the back when you least expect it. Many people would rather deal with Bill Gates's frontal assaults.

One of those who knows all about both the difficulties and rewards of dealing with Bill Gates is Andy Grove, the head of the chip manufacturer Intel. Grove, nineteen years older than Gates, was born in Hungary, where he survived the Nazi horrors of a World War II childhood only to find himself living under the yoke of Stalinism. He was twenty when he escaped to the west after the 1956 Hungarian uprising, eventually getting a Ph.D. from the University of California at Berkeley. He and Gates first met when Allen and Gates dropped by to introduce themselves in 1978, when Microsoft was still located in Albuquerque. Two years later, giant IBM hired Intel to provide the chips and Microsoft to create the software as they tried to play catch-up with Apple in the new field of personal computers.

There were some rough patches between the two men early on. In a 1996 joint interview, they told *Fortune* about a dinner at Groves's home that turned into a table-pounding shouting match. Groves recalled, "It was not a pleasant evening. I remember the caterer peeked into the room to see what all the ruckus was about. I was the only one who finished my salmon." For a while after that Groves and

The other day someone asked me, "Can't Microsoft work with people so that they can be successful too?" That night I looked at a chart comparing Intel's valuation with our valuation over the years. Although they vary somewhat, in both cases they went from a relatively small number to a relatively gigantic number. And I thought, "When have there ever been two companies with that kind of dependency both rising to that kind of success?" Even though we can tell you about all these disagreements and sarcastic meetings, we haven't really gotten in each other's way all that much. To me, that's really amazing.

—Bill Gates, in a joint *Fortune* interview with
Intel CEO Andy Grove, 1996

Gates had contact only through other representatives of their two companies. But they got past that period and began to meet on a regular basis, two or three times a year, as their companies became more and more entwined with one another on many developmental projects. In part, they were drawn together because IBM broke with both of them. IBM invested in Intel, but sold its last interest in the company in 1987; it had refused to invest in Microsoft the previous year. "As these things happened," Grove said, "instead of being two junior partners of a senior partner, we became equal players without that senior partner being present."

The results of the relationship between the two companies have been profoundly beneficial to both, and have been instrumental in keeping computer development moving ahead at an extraordinary pace. The two men have continued to have disagreements on many issues, but they have usually proved to be fruitful ones. Both men acknowledge that they get input from different sources. This sometimes causes friction, but more often it leads to showing each other the best way forward in an area that one or the other has failed to grasp clearly. Gates and Grove also are very complimentary about one another's companies. Gates says, "It's fun to hear Intel's plans, because when they decide to do a next-generation processor, the execution is amazing. There's so much behind it in terms of capital and design and testing and the like." Grove returns the compliment: "What I'm most impressed with about Microsoft is that they are superb tacticians. They zigzag very, very well . . . if they are wrong they can be very, very pragmatic. What they are doing in the Internet field is phenomenal. I don't think any other large company could have turned as profoundly and as broadly . . ."

The IBM lesson is cautionary to us. Almost every day we say, "Have we become them?"

—BILL GATES, *Newsweek,* 1996

This is not to say that they wouldn't decide to work with a different partner if someone came up with better chips than Intel, or better software than Microsoft. They tend to agree that the PC and the television set will merge, and that the network computer or Internet terminal, cheaper and simpler and being pushed hard by Larry Ellison of Oracle, will fall between stools. But if things go the other way and Oracle's vision of the future proves correct, it is perfectly possible that Microsoft and Intel might find themselves at odds in dealing with that development. Microsoft's continued success depends on the ongoing dominance of the PC, even though Gates has made recent investments in a few companies that could give him an escape hatch. But Intel, as a chip maker, is in the more flexible position. Whatever new technology arises, it will need chips; it might not need Windows. But regardless of what happens, Gates and Grove are in agreement that the synergy that has existed between their two companies has been remarkable and close to unique since the start of the industrial revolution more than two centuries ago.

The relationship between Bill Gates and Andy Grove shows the degree to which Gates can be cooperative when there is a common ground. But it is worth noting that the two businesses are complementary rather than competitive with one another. In this sense, the relationship mirrors Gates's personal life. His closest friends are, with one exception, people intimately tied to Microsoft: cofounder Paul Allen, Steve Ballmer, who keeps everything running smoothly, and Nathan Myhrvold, head of Microsoft's Advanced Research Division and a coauthor of *The Road Ahead*. The exception, of course, is Warren Buffett, older than Gates and nearly as rich, who has almost nothing to do with the computer world. He bought a few shares of

Information is any sort of data that's out there. Knowledge? Everybody has their own opinion of what's most important and therefore what's worth focusing on.

—BILL GATES, on the information highway, 1995

Microsoft early on and laughs that he should have bought a lot more, but his primary investments are in other fields. Perhaps exactly because Buffett is not a part of the frenetic computer society, Gates may be at his most relaxed and playful with this billionaire who is neither a collaborator nor a competitor.

Having a friend from outside the computer industry to relax with probably seemed particularly felicitous to Gates in the fall of 1997, when a number of business problems coalesced. On September 15, Microsoft confirmed rumors that the latest version of its operating system software, Windows 98, would be delayed from the first to the second quarter of 1998. While Windows 95 had been nearly two years late, this fresh announcement caused Microsoft stock to fall by five percent that day, with a share falling by $7.25, although its stock still stood at fifty times the company's earnings and rallied the following day. Windows 98, it had been announced previously, would include Microsoft's browser, Internet Explorer, as an integral part of Windows for the first time. That plan would shortly be challenged on two separate fronts.

On October 7, 1997, Sun Microsystems, Inc. filed a suit in the Federal District Court of San Jose, California, charging that Microsoft was essentially attempting to "steal" Sun's Java software standard by including a conflicting version of that software language in its new Internet Explorer 4.0 browser program. Microsoft had licensed the use of the Java language in April of 1996, four months after it was released by Sun, after five months of negotiation. Java is a programming language at base, but its design also allows it to be used as an all-purpose computer operating system—in other words, a potential alternative to Windows. Because it can run a wide range of different computer sys-

What's new about Java versus other programming languages? Why is *Business Week* writing about Java? Just having another computer language doesn't change the dynamic of these things.

—BILL GATES, bad-mouthing Java to *Business Week*, even though he had authorized talks about licensing the new language from Sun Microsystems, late 1995

tems, Java was intended to bypass vexing compatability problems in the computer industry—indeed, Sun touted it with the phrase "Write once, run anywhere." In addition, it was designed to mitigate security problems, particularly those caused by viruses, on computer network systems. Because Java can run on almost any system, it is not necessary to have the kind of extended linkage that makes a whole network vulnerable.

Sun has been attempting to have Java adopted as an international standard, a move that industry analysts have seen as a threat to the domination of Microsoft's Windows operating system, since Java lessens the need for Windows in several important areas, including the retrieval of information from the Internet. What's more, a Microsoft application like Word could be used with Java instead of with Windows. In developing its Internet Explorer 4.0, therefore, Windows changed the Java language to make it less versatile, removing two crucial standards established by Sun. That, Sun maintained in its suit, was a violation of the licensing agreement. Microsoft, of course, said that it had not violated anything at all and that it had also made improvements to the Java standard that Sun had not yet gotten around to making but that were beneficial to all computer users. Exactly because Java is so broadly compatible, it is open to improvement by customization to a specific operating system like Windows. Microsoft made some forty changes over all, which simultaneously made Java more useful to Windows users but less compatible with other software products from rival companies. The *New York Times* quoted David Yoffie, a professor at the Harvard Business School, as saying that "Microsoft's optimization is a risk for Sun. But if Sun can slow down Microsoft's

. . . Microsoft was clearly behind, which was an opportunity for other companies to get ahead. By enabling Microsoft to better compete, we had effectively closed that window of opportunity for those other companies. We gave Microsoft some very important keys to the castle. But in our defense, we saw this as good for Java. It was better to work with Microsoft than not. And eventually they would have built a Java clone. We had heard rumors that one was already in the works.

—Eric Schmidt, Sun's chief technology officer,
on licensing Java to Microsoft, December 1995

advances with the software developers, this will prove to be a good strategy."

It may well take years for the Sun lawsuit to be decided; many computer industry suits consume two to five years of legal maneuvering. In the meantime, Sun and other Microsoft rivals were bending ears at the Justice Department, trying to persuade the Antitrust Division to take new action against Gates's company. Even Ralph Nader, the legendary consumer activist, got into the act in September 1997, holding a much publicized meeting with top Justice Department officials. The director of Nader's Consumer Project on Technology said at that time, "We think it's an outrage that the Justice Department hasn't taken action to stop Microsoft." Spokespeople from Microsoft immediately professed astonishment that Nader would go after a company that had worked so hard to improve software technology while at the same time lowering the prices consumers paid for it.

While considering the possibility of new actions against Microsoft in various areas, the Justice Department took a major step on Monday, October 20, 1997, to reassure those who had been filing complaints about Microsoft. In a news conference given by Attorney General Janet Reno and Joel I. Klein, assistant attorney general for the Antitrust Division, who had been confirmed by the Senate in July, it was announced that the Justice Department had filed a complaint in federal court stating that Microsoft was in violation of the 1995 consent decree it had signed with the federal government and had asked the court to stop Microsoft from bundling Internet Explorer, its browser, with the Windows 95 operating system. The presence of Janet Reno at the news conference ensured headlines, but what really got the attention of the media was the request by the Justice

It's kind of funny that it's the computer industry, where the prices come down and the products get better and nobody has a guaranteed position, that's the one that somebody would look into.

—BILL GATES, on Ralph Nader's attack on Microsoft, 1997

Department that once such an order was issued by the court, Microsoft should be fined $1 million a day until it complied.

The one-million-dollar-a-day potential fine made for splashy headlines, but it was quickly pointed out that although a fine of such proportions would be unprecedented, it would still be a drop in the bucket to Microsoft. Several commentators used the phrase "chump change" to describe what a million a day was to Gates, and *Newsweek* noted that in the days following the announcement of the Justice Department complaint, Microsoft stock went up three points, adding $846 million to Gates's own net worth. Moreover, Gates himself indicated that such a fine was unnecessary, since Microsoft would comply immediately with whatever the court ordered. "That's the way things work in this country," he said.

But even leaving aside the matter of the possible fine, the action by the Justice Department was an aggressive challenge to Microsoft. The crux of the complaint was that Microsoft was forcing PC manufacturers to include its Internet Explorer on all new computers or lose the right to install Windows 95. The most damaging testimony was collected from Stephen Decker, the director of software procurement at the top PC manufacturer Compaq. Decker told Justice Department antitrust attorneys that in the spring of 1996 Compaq had wanted to put the icon for Netscape Navigator on its desktop instead of the icon for Microsoft's Internet Explorer. Both browsers would continue to be available on the new PCs, but since it was assumed that computer buyers knew that the Microsoft browser was always included, Compaq wanted to make it clear that the rival Netscape system was included also. At that point, the Microsoft browser, which had been introduced a year later

A fundamental principle at Microsoft is that Windows gets better and makes the PC easier to use with each new version. Today people want to use PCs to access the Internet. We are providing that functionality in Windows, and providing a platform for innovation by thousands of other software companies. It would be a great disservice to our customers if Microsoft did not enhance Windows with Internet-related features and rapidly distribute updated versions of Windows through PC manufacturers.

—BILL GATES, initial response to the Justice Department action, October 20, 1997

than Netscape's, had only four percent of the browser market, while Netscape's had eighty-seven percent. The much greater popularity of the Netscape product at that time also made it the more enticing icon to have displayed. But Microsoft got tough on this intended move—fast. It informed Compaq that it was terminating its Windows 95 licensing agreement with Compaq. A few days later it said that it would reconsider if Compaq replaced the Microsoft Internet Explorer within sixty days.

It would, of course, have been ruinous for Compaq not to have been able to ship the world's foremost operating system, Windows 95, and it quickly complied. By August of that year, the market share of Microsoft's browser doubled to eight percent, with the added points coming directly from Netscape's browser, which dropped to eighty-three percent, while the share of smaller rivals remained at nine percent. And by September of 1997, Microsoft had acquired thirty-six percent of the browser market, Netscape was down to sixty-two percent, and the small rivals were left with only two percent of the market. To Janet Reno and antitrust head Joel Klein that was clear evidence that the pressure applied to Compaq (which had been duly noted by other PC manufacturers) had directly harmed Netscape and amounted to Microsoft "unlawfully taking advantage of its Windows monopoly to protect and extend that monopoly and undermine consumer choice," as Janet Reno put it. At the October 20, 1997 news conference Reno added that the Justice Department "won't tolerate any coercion by dominant companies in any way that distorts competition."

The question of whether Microsoft had in fact violated its 1995 consent decree depended on whether or not its browser was considered an entirely separate product from

If you're asking for a guarantee that your company will be successful, then you are in the wrong business. We put into the operating system the things a super-high percentage of our customers want and keep the price of Windows very aggressive . . . in this business every year you have to prove yourself.

—BILL GATES, at a computer industry conference in Scottsdale, Arizona, the day after the Justice Department filing, October 21, 1997

Windows 95 or an integrated part of it. If it was an integrated aspect of Windows, then the consent decree hadn't been violated, most analysts agreed. But if it was an independent product that Microsoft had forced PC manufacturers to accept in order to ship their computers with Windows, then the decree had been violated. From the point of view of Netscape, as put forward to *Time* by Netscape general counsel Roberta Katz, it was unequivocally a separate product: "They've produced it as a separate product. They've advertised it separately; they've produced it separately; they've sold it separately."

But there is a weakness in this statement that some analysts took note of: Microsoft's Internet browser is *free*. Microsoft does not charge PC manufacturers to install it—they just insist that it be installed. In addition, from the beginning, computer users could download it free if their computer did not already have it. Can a company really be accused of coercion when the product in question is a giveaway? The commonsense answer to that question is no. But to Microsoft's competitors, the answer is, Wait and see if it's still free once Microsoft has cornered the market. Ralph Nader hit hard on this point, saying that the fact that Internet Explorer is now free "is a classic definition of predatory pricing. Once they get rid of Netscape you will see the difference."

But can Microsoft really knock Netscape out of the browser business? The technical analysts don't think so. Independent computer publications like *PC Magazine*, as well as Wall Street technical analysts, feel that the Microsoft and Netscape products have different strengths and weaknesses, and that the choice of one over the other may depend on what a user wants to do in terms of accessing the Internet. In a November 1997 editorial, Michael J.

Who should determine what's in Windows? It's what the consumers want. There is nothing else.

—BILL GATES, October 1997

Miller, editor of *PC Magazine*, flatly said, "I think you should have both browsers on your system." What's more, analysts who specialize in looking ahead suggest that both browsers may be only temporary solutions to accessing the Internet. There are several start-up companies, some with considerable financial support from major corporations that have a stake in the future of the Internet, that are concentrating on the development of set-top boxes for television sets. Such set-top boxes would make it possible for users to access the Internet using remote controls no more complicated than those used for VCRs, with the real computing done at central networks leased to local television cable companies. That eventuality, it is pointed out, is far more of a threat to Microsoft than any Justice Department confrontation, since the Internet would then be available to people who don't even own a PC, and who would have no need for Windows at all.

The current Justice Department challenge to Microsoft is unlikely to take such future developments into account, however. It will call upon the court to weigh the fact that Microsoft clearly twisted the arms of PC manufacturers, as shown in the Compaq situation, against the fact that Microsoft's Internet Explorer is free anyway. It will also turn on the history of Microsoft's development of its browser. Because Microsoft delayed the rollout of Windows 95 for nearly a year in order to change it in ways that would make it possible for users to also use the Internet Explorer, a case will certainly be made by Gates and his lawyers that the browser was thus integral to Windows even though it will not become a technically subsumed part of the operating system until the advent of Windows 98. At a deeper, but perhaps more important, level, the case will have to deal with the ever-changing nature of

Are we allowed to continue to innovate in products, and in Windows itself?

—BILL GATES, on the real question, as he sees it, about integrating Microsoft's browser, October 1997

Microsoft is a great white shark that knows no boundaries. All it knows is its appetite. When it gets hungry, it eats.

—MICHAEL KERTZMAN, CEO of Sybase, giving the view of many Microsoft competitors, October 1997

My style is, I am careful.

—JOEL KLEIN, head of the Justice Department Antitrust Division, October 1997

computers and computer software, and face the question of whether it makes good sense or good law to prohibit a company from continually enhancing its products to meet the needs of users in an increasingly computerized world. When it comes to that issue, even Microsoft's bitterest rivals get nervous. They want to see Bill Gates and Microsoft controlled by the government (even damaged), but they don't want a decision that will inhibit their own ability to create and sell ever more useful products.

CHAPTER SIX

THE MICROSOFT/APPLE STORY

It's a great machine. It allows us to write software which is significantly easy to use. . . . There's no way this group could have done any of this stuff without Jobs.

—BILL GATES, on the upcoming Macintosh and Steve Jobs's part in developing it, to Steve Levy of *Newsweek*, 1983

Although the importance of Bill Gates and Microsoft to the computer industry is evident in his relationship with collaborators like Andy Grove and detractors such as Scott McNealy, the extraordinary clout that Gates and his company have achieved is most clearly seen in the complex relationship between Microsoft and Apple. The two companies have been linked by far-reaching business agreements since the early 1980s, when both companies first broke out of the pack of fledgling enterprises that were attempting to shape the future of the personal computer industry. But despite these links, the two companies have also been seriously at odds with one another on many fronts. The ups and downs of their relationship reveal the degree to which interdependence can arise between rivals in the computer industry, creating a complex web of crisscrossing loyalties and oppositions that many experts say is like nothing ever seen before in an industrial or technological field.

In 1977, when Steve Jobs and Steve Wozniak unveiled the Apple I personal computer, Bill Gates and Paul Allen were still operating out of a strip mall in Albuquerque, New Mexico. By 1980, Apple II had become a big enough success to goad IBM into changing its tune about the future of the personal computer; it contacted Microsoft to develop an operating system for the PC it had in development. But at that point, few people outside the computer industry had any idea who Bill Gates was. It was Steve Jobs and Apple that were getting the cover stories. Apple became a public company in December 1980, selling 4.6 million shares of stock at the initial offering price of $22 per share. But nine months later, in September of 1981, IBM began shipping its PCs, and their new product quickly eclipsed the sales of the Apple II. Even the upgrade to the Apple

Microsoft bet the company on graphical interfaces. . . . It took much longer than I expected for the graphics interface to move into the mainstream, but today we can say that it is the dominant way that people use their personal computer. We can just look at the sales of DOS applications as compared to Windows applications and see that, over the last two and a half years, character-based applications have gone from being about eighty percent of the market to now less than twenty percent.

—BILL GATES, in a speech at Boston Computer Society, October 1993

IIe in 1983 wasn't enough to stem the flood of IBM PCs and its clones.

Part of the problem was that Apple was developing both the hardware and the software for its personal computers. As IBM itself would subsequently discover after Microsoft pulled out of its relationship with IBM because of differences about the development of OS/2 operating software, when a single company is producing both software and hardware, especially in the fast-changing PC world, the hardware forces at the company tend to have the upper hand when it comes to disagreements about how to proceed. Thus when Jobs decided that the way to counter the IBM surge was to develop not simply a new computer but an entirely new kind of operating system, he sought out Bill Gates to share in the development of the software. What they produced together was a revolutionary approach. As Steve Levy wrote in *Newsweek* in August of 1997, "The antidote was Macintosh. People scarcely remember now, but the Mac was a drastic change from all previous PCs. Some people believed that its on-screen graphics made it too toylike to be a business tool; others vowed they would never use that strange device called a mouse." But it was the future of PCs. Jobs was certain of it, and Gates, who at one point had more Microsoft programmers at work on Mac software than Apple itself, agreed. In fact, Gates had such a clear sense of the importance of the graphical interface that he set his own company on the path to developing a similar operating system that could be used on the PCs sold by IBM and the companies it had licensed to produce IBM clones. The Microsoft operating system would be called Windows.

By taking this step, Gates put Microsoft in the position of being both the chief supplier of Apple's Macintosh soft-

You have to remember when you talk about Macintosh, Microsoft still makes more money for every Macintosh that ships than for every PC that ships. We have a higher market share of Word and Excel on the Macintosh than we will ever have in the Windows environment. So the fact that the Mac is a machine that lots of people use in mixed environments is great news for us. We are an open company. We're open to whatever desktop platforms are popular.

—BILL GATES, January 1993

ware and, in time, the chief supplier of software to Apple's hardware competitors. As Michael A. Cusumano and Richard W. Selby make clear in the appendix to their book, *Microsoft Secrets*, there is an enormous overlap between the Windows software and the software developed for Macintosh. For example, Microsoft's two "flagship" application products, the spreadsheet Excel and the word processor Word, each of which accounts for a billion dollars a year in Microsoft sales, share "80 to 85 percent" of their code with products produced for Macintosh. Cusumano and Selby's book is not only sympathetic to Microsoft (despite its somewhat sinister title) but it was also written with Microsoft's blessing—the authors enjoyed unprecedented access to Microsoft personnel. Gates himself answered the author's question, Why let us write this book? by saying, "It's good for our corporate customers to know more about development because they do a lot of development. In aggregate, they have a lot more developers than the commercial software industry does. And so we want to remind them that we have some good ideas, and share those ideas with them. Maybe they'll buy more PCs."

Behind these words lies Gates's conviction that there is nothing at all wrong with the fact that Microsoft's products for Macintosh and for Windows share more than two-thirds of their code. Apple had of course agreed to allow Microsoft to use code developed for Macintosh in creating its own software for other PC manufacturers. After all, IBM had already done the same thing. And Gates, who always took the long view, would not collaborate under any other terms. It is worth noting that Apple had already become a publicly held company, with its initial stock offering of December 1980, before Microsoft even incorporated, which it did not do until 1981. What's more, Microsoft was not

Our most successful software is for the Macintosh. We have a much higher market share on the Mac than anywhere else. How does Apple help us? Well, they sue us in court. In the future, maybe our competitors will decide to become more competent.

—BILL GATES, June 1993

listed on the New York Stock Exchange until 1986. It was not until Microsoft's stock became a Wall Street favorite, outstripping Apple, that Apple began to seriously complain about the overlap between Windows and Macintosh software.

In the meantime, Steve Jobs found himself ousted from Apple. His charisma, enthusiasm, and public relations genius had made Apple what it was, but he was not a financial expert, and in April of 1983 he persuaded the president of Pepsi-Cola, John Sculley, to become head of Apple. Their relationship proved combative, and when Apple posted its first quarterly loss in September of 1985 and Jobs failed in an attempt to force the board to get rid of Sculley, he left the company he had founded.

Jobs and Gates had understood one another, despite some differences. Sculley saw Gates as the enemy, even though Apple remained dependent on software produced by Microsoft. In 1988, Apple filed suit against Microsoft for copyright infringement, citing the newly released Windows 2.03 for making use of code that was Apple's property. While Bill Gates has noted caustically that there are *always* several dozen suits pending against Microsoft, this new Apple challenge asked for $5 billion in damages and had to be treated with great seriousness.

The case involved both code and the use of the mouse to click on to a graphical user interface (GUI). In the course of developing the original Macintosh GUI, Microsoft developers, as Cusumano and Selby note, "became intimately familiar with the Mac's user interface and internal workings." The contract between Apple and Microsoft gave Apple only minimal protection against the possibility that Microsoft would develop its own GUI, preventing it from doing so for one year after the initial shipment of the Mac-

It's only through volume that you can offer reasonable software at a low price. . . . I really shouldn't say this, but in some ways it leads, in an individual product category, to a natural monopoly: where somebody properly documents, properly trains, properly promotes a particular package and through momentum, user loyalty, reputation, sales force, and prices builds a very strong position with that product.

—BILL GATES, staking out an early defense on the monopoly issue, 1981

intosh. After that, Macintosh was supposedly free to move ahead on its own. But Apple believed that Windows 2.03 emulated the "look and feel" of the Macintosh interface too closely.

The suit was contested for four years, during which time Microsoft released Windows 3.0 (May 1990) and Apple unveiled its PowerBook laptop, both great successes for their respective companies. Microsoft finally got the Apple suit dismissed in April of 1992, in part by arguing that the graphical interface technology did not even belong to Apple but had been invented by the Xerox team at its Palo Alto Research Center, known as PARC. The PARC team had not been able to figure out how to make the technology commercially available, however. In dismissing Apple's suit against Microsoft, the federal judge in the case, Vaughn Walker, ruled that Microsoft had already licensed some of the technology, and that other similarities could not be covered by copyright. As James Wallace puts it in *Overdrive*, "A ruling in favor of Apple's claims, the judge said, would have 'afforded too much protection and yielded too little competition.' This not only vindicated Microsoft, it was also significant for the industry, clearing away doubts about the rights of software programmers to adapt aspects of other systems." This legal victory had by that time cost Microsoft $9 million in legal fees.

The relationship between Apple and Microsoft had been further strained by another kind of problem. As far back as 1987, Microsoft had earned the everlasting enmity of many Macintosh users by producing a bug-ridden version of its Word 3.0 for Macintosh. Not only were there as many as seven hundred bugs but some of them were so serious that they crashed the program completely. Even though Microsoft spent a million dollars shipping an up-

Some readers implore Microsoft to make its applications, such as Microsoft Word and Microsoft Excel, available on computing platforms such as Amiga and OS/2. Adapting applications to work on additional platforms is expensive. In the early years of OS/2, we created a lot of applications for it, and although we were the market leader, we didn't sell very many and it wasn't profitable. That's why Microsoft, like almost all other successful software companies, focuses its resources on Windows and the Macintosh.

—BILL GATES, 1995

grade two months later, the suspicion was planted in the minds of Macintosh users that Bill Gates regarded them as second-class citizens. That impression was furthered in 1993 when Mac Word 6.0 proved to be slow and cumbersome. Once again, an upgrade, in this case a trimmed-down one, had to be shipped. It was incidents of this kind that virtually assured the appearance on the Internet, as it developed in the mid-1990s, of virulent anti-Gates and anti-Microsoft web sites, which have always been much visited by Macintosh devotees.

The anti-Microsoft bias on the part of Macintosh users only grew in the mid-1990s as Microsoft extended its grip on the computer industry with Windows 95, while Apple encountered more and more difficulties. In 1993, Apple unveiled a new product, the handheld Newton computer, which was disparaged from the word go and was a complete commercial flop. In the wake of that disaster, John Sculley was deposed, and Michael Spindler was brought in as CEO. A German, he was nicknamed "the Deisel," but as *Newsweek* reported, his "regime was more like a train wreck." Among the other problems on his watch was a parts shortage for the new Power Macintosh of 1994, which created a billion dollars in back orders.

One positive step taken during Spindler's term was to license the manufacture of Macintosh clones by other companies. This was a step that many industry analysts had been recommending for years; indeed, Gates had formally suggested it as far back as 1985, offering to assist in such a move. IBM had allowed such clones of its PC from the start and benefited greatly, but Apple had always had a strong resistance to surrendering what it saw as its unique identity. By the time the step was finally taken in 1994, many observers felt it was too late.

The Mac is an excellent platform. Apple, like every high-technology company, must continue to innovate. If it does, it will do well—and we'll do well selling applications software for the Mac.

—BILL GATES, 1995

Apple losses were growing steadily when Spindler was replaced in February of 1996 by Gil Amelio, who had a reputation as a "turnaround" expert. A nervous board of directors tried to find a buyer for Apple, but such companies as IBM, AT&T, and Sun proved to be extremely skittish about such a deal. Apple had been promising a new, revolutionary operating system, but its development was in serious trouble. In order to get it jump-started, Amelio decided to purchase NeXT, a company that had been started by Steve Jobs after leaving Apple, and to integrate the NeXT technology with Apple's. Jobs had become more interested in another company he owned, the computer animation firm Pixar, which had had a major hit with its new process in the movie *Toy Story*. Jobs thus agreed to sell NeXT for $430 million.

The acquisition of NeXT took place in December 1996, but the board soon after decided that Amelio was not the right person for Apple, and he departed in July of 1997. While searching for a new CEO, the board turned to Steve Jobs to informally oversee Apple in the interim. Jobs insisted that he did not want to once again head the company he had founded, but he did take a strong hand in developing a new strategy. Despite the company's financial and developmental problems, it still had a number of strengths. The user-friendly Macintosh remained the computer of choice in the world of education, not only among students but also with educators themselves. In the first quarter of 1997, according to figures compiled by Dataquest, Apple's share of computer sales to the U.S. education market were 29.6 percent, three times that of its closest competitor, Dell, at 9.6 percent, with several other companies close behind. Its graphic software also remained the favorite among computer graphic designers, with its presentation software hav-

Develop for it? I'll piss on it.

—BILL GATES, responding to a question about developing software
for Steve Job's NeXT technology in the mid-1990s, as reported by
John Heilemann in the *New Yorker*

ing a 51.6 percent market share and its drawing and painting software a 43.9 percent share, according to PC Data. Its share of overall desktop publishing software was even higher in these markets, at 62.4 percent.

But there were danger signs even in these markets. At Yale University, for example, according to an article in the *New York Times,* seventy-five percent of the class of 1997 had been Macintosh users, but only twenty-five percent of the class of 2000 were when they entered the university in 1996. What's more, in June of 1997, a letter to incoming freshmen advised that they purchase computers that were equipped with Intel microprocessors and Windows operating systems. "The University cannot guarantee support for Macintoshes beyond June 2000," the letter bluntly stated. This letter developed into a small scandal when it was subsequently learned that the university had applied for a several million dollar research grant from Intel. Yale said there was no connection between the two events, but even so, the negative statements about the Macintosh drew many protests. Regardless of that particular situation, the drop in the number of Macintosh users was a sign of serious trouble for Apple.

When Steve Jobs returned to Apple as an all-powerful "adviser," he found that the company was planning another copyright infringement suit against Microsoft, this time in connection with Windows 95. Neither side really wanted another court battle like the one that had lasted from 1988 to 1992, but Amelio had asked for what Gates regarded as excessive terms to avoid a suit. Jobs quickly approached Gates about finding a way to settle the matter. Gates dispatched Greg Maffei, Microsoft's chief financial officer, to deal with Jobs face-to-face. Negotiations went on during the last two weeks of July and into August of 1997.

We think Apple makes a huge contribution to the computer industry.

—BILL GATES, speaking to the Macworld Expo in Boston following the announcement of Microsoft's $150 million investment in Apple

If there was to be a deal, Jobs wanted to announce it at the Macworld Expo to be held in Boston, Massachusetts, the second week of August. But a very tight lid was kept on the possibility of a deal. No one expected the announcement that Jobs was to make on Wednesday, August 6.

The hall in which the announcement was made was dominated by an enormous screen that, as numerous commentators pointed out, was eerily reminiscent of the screen used in the famous "1984" commercial that had launched the Macintosh. The scene became stranger still as the screen filled with the towering face of Bill Gates, joining in from Redmond, Washington, to share with Jobs the announcement that Microsoft was investing $150 million in Apple. The sixteen hundred die-hard Macintosh fans in the audience couldn't believe what was happening. Moments earlier, they had given Jobs a rousing standing ovation when he walked on stage. Now they were booing and catcalling the image of Bill Gates. Their initial reaction suggested that they thought Jobs had made a deal with the Devil himself.

As several members of that audience told the press afterwards, the Apple mythology had over the years turned Bill Gates into a figure inspiring both fear and loathing. And now he was on their side? But up on the screen that's exactly what he was saying. The antagonistic crowd quickly realized that in fact this announcement might actually be Apple's salvation. At the very least it would give the company a transfusion of cash—and even more important, credibility—that would prolong its life. And here they were booing the life-giving donor. What's more, it occurred to them, Bill Gates could hear them booing, all the way out on the Pacific coast. This wasn't a video they were looking up at but a two-way hookup. Applause began, and the crowd settled back to listen.

We want to let go of this notion that for Apple to win, Microsoft has to lose. We better treat Microsoft with a little gratitude.

—STEVE JOBS, chiding the Macworld audience that jeered the live image of Bill Gates in Boston, 1997

"Understand," Cathy Booth wrote in *Time*, "the idea of Jobs returning to Apple is something akin to that of Luke Skywalker returning to fight what, until last week, cultists regarded as the evil empire. Gates, by comparison, was perceived as a dweeb Darth Vader, the billionaire bad guy who usurped the idea of the Macintosh's friendly point and click operating system for his now dominant Windows."

But by the next day the shock had worn off, and most Macintosh devotees were focusing on the good news. Apple stock had whizzed upward by 33 percent in the wake of the announcement, to $26.31. That was still only about one-tenth of the value of Microsoft stock, of course, but it was a vast improvement over what had been a long decline—one that had begun with the August 1995 release of Windows 95. Back then, Apple computers had held a 10.3 percent share of the market. They were now down to a 3.5 percent share. Many had predicted that the end was in sight for the company, but with Microsoft's investment, it could now be said with some credibility that the company would find a way to survive. It wasn't the amount of money that mattered, analysts almost unanimously agreed. After all, $150 million was nothing more than "loose change," as some put it, to Microsoft, with its $9 billion in cash on hand. But it was a sign that Microsoft did not want to see Apple go under, and the fact that Microsoft was buying nonvoting stock meant that Bill Gates wasn't going to be running Apple on the side.

But as Steve Jobs spent the next day pointing out to reporters, the big news wasn't the $150 million investment, anyway. The big news was that Microsoft was paying an undisclosed sum to Apple to close the books on Apple's charges of copyright infringement. This was not a matter

We at no time, in any way, have threatened to stop developing for the Macintosh. I don't even understand what it would mean. It's the most bizarre thing in the world. What would we get out of that. It's a big revenue source. It's a profitable business.

—BILL GATES, in an interview with *Time*, dismissing a rumor leaked by Apple, 1995

of Microsoft admitting it had done anything wrong, of course—it was simply getting a bitter disagreement that could cost both companies endless litigation fees, with all the bad publicity such suits entail, out of the way of future cooperation.

The agreement between Apple and Microsoft had been front-page news, and the weekly magazines carried cover stories on the deal the following week. Steve Jobs was in the limelight as he hadn't been since the early 1980s. The media focused on his part in the deal more than it did on Bill Gates. But even in the newsweeklies, there were already those who were suggesting that putting Steve Jobs out in front on this deal suited Bill Gates's plans exactly. *Newsweek*'s Wall Street editor Allan Sloan had a full-page commentary titled "Bill does what's good for Bill." This wasn't in itself a headline that would surprise anyone. But the subtitle for Sloan's article read, "Microsoft needs Apple to ward off trustbusters." According to this view, which was echoed in many quarters, for Gates to be seen as coming to Apple's rescue buttressed his stand that Microsoft was not the industry villain but had the best interests of the overall advancement of computer technology at heart. The demise of Apple would only have raised an even greater outcry to the effect that Gates was a greedy monopolist on the scale of such earlier operators as John D. Rockefeller. For Gates to appear to come to Apple's rescue would have the opposite effect. As detailed earlier, this strategy— if it was in fact central to Gates's thinking in the first place—did not work. A little more than two months later, Attorney General Janet Reno would announce that the Justice Department was seeking a federal judge's order to prevent Microsoft from "bundling" its Internet Explorer with Windows, a practice that the Justice Department found to

Thank you for your support of this company. I
think the world's a better place for it.

—STEVE JOBS to BILL GATES, via cell phone, the day before the big
announcement, August 5, 1997

be in violation of the 1995 consent agreement between Microsoft and the government.

But in August commentators also pointed to another reason why the Apple deal was "good for Bill." The sales of Macintosh software produced by Microsoft account for several times $150 million in income to Microsoft each year, even with a much weakened Macintosh market. Why not spend some money to keep that income flowing, commentators asked? It would be foolish to do otherwise. There were also suggestions that Microsoft, having bought its shares of Apple stock at around $16.50, according to Allan Sloan, stood to gain back a major part of its investment on the ensuing rise in the value of Apple stock. Sloan put the Microsoft paper profit for the two days following the deal at $90 million. But that was not simply a paper profit; it was an ephemeral one. Apple stock was soon down several points, and by mid-October it had dropped out of the twenties altogether.

In the long run, what would happen to Apple would depend upon its own ability to streamline and innovate its business. Steve Jobs managed to install an almost entirely new board during the summer of 1997, including one of Bill Gates's longtime antagonists, Larry Ellison of Oracle, who had floated the idea that he might buy Apple back in March of 1997. Ellison then backed off, serving to further undermine the tenure of Gil Amelio. John Heilemann reported in the *New Yorker* that the inclusion of Ellison on the board had given Microsoft considerable pause—"That took us some time to get comfortable with," Microsoft's Greg Maffei told Heilemann.

Beyond getting a better board, there remained the major question of what new directions Apple should take in developing future products. One possibility was to cre-

And we welcome Microsoft to the family of Apple investors. But more important than any of that, I think our goal was to normalize the relationships with Microsoft so we could get on with doing business together. As I said at Macworld, Apple plus Microsoft equals 100 percent of the desktop markets. There are no other players. . . . It's not that Apple is going to become like Microsoft; they're obviously going to continue to compete. But it's crazy for the only two players in the desktop market not to be working together. It's a little like Nixon going to China. It's the right thing to do.

—STEVE JOBS to *Newsweek* after the announcement of the new Apple/Microsoft alliance, August 1997

ate Rhapsody, an operating system for businesses, using the NeXT software originally developed by Jobs's own company, with Apple development work. But Gates had always been dubious about NeXT and about Apple's attempt to attract business customers who had never been enthusiastic about the Macintosh.

According to John Heilemann and other commentators, the Apple deal was particularly appealing to Gates because it would commit Apple to using Microsoft's Internet Explorer on future Macintoshes, rather than the rival Internet browser developed earlier by Netscape. That Microsoft advantage could, of course, be scuttled by the Justice Department's attack on the bundling of Internet Explorer. Heilemann notes that Gates also wanted to develop "his own version of Java, tailored to Windows." Java, created by Sun Systems to run on all operating systems, is seen by many analysts as representing the future of the Internet. Heilemann says that the Microsoft/Apple deal "commits Apple, in effect, to helping Gates" develop a Java language for Windows. But that, too, may prove difficult. In October 1997, Sun filed a lawsuit to prevent Microsoft from doing so.

Thus the eventual benefits of the new alliance between Microsoft and Apple remain in question for both companies. At the same time, the initial announcement of their renewed closeness provides a dramatic new twist to a relationship, sometimes beneficial and sometimes acrimonious, that goes back to the start of the PC revolution and involves the two names—Gates and Jobs—that have the most resonance with the general public in terms of the computer industry.

CHAPTER SEVEN

THE PERSONAL SIDE

Sometimes people ask me what field I'd be in if I were not in computers. I think I'd be working in biotechnology. I expect to see breathtaking advances in medicine over the next two decades, and biotechnology researchers and companies will be at the center of that progress. I'm a big believer in information technology and the way it is revolutionizing how people work, play, and learn. But it's hard to argue that the emerging medical revolution, spearheaded by the biotechnology industry, is any less important to the future of humankind.

—BILL GATES, 1996

The CEOs who run America's most powerful companies are not usually well known to the general public. There are legendary names that linger from the past—Andrew Carnegie, John D. Rockefeller, Henry Ford—but only a few current names are recognized by ordinary Americans. Media moguls predominate, including Rupert Murdoch, Ted Turner, and Disney's Michael Eisner. Every era has its publicity-seeking businessmen like Donald Trump, who contrive to be better known than they are important. But by and large, the heads of the companies that so greatly influence our daily lives manage to remain somewhat anonymous. They may get the occasional magazine cover, but they avoid the steady drumbeat of publicity that makes someone a household name. There are some people, like Lee Iacocca and Frank Purdue in the 1980s, who become so associated with their company's products by appearing in television ads that it's almost impossible to avoid knowing who they are. But few could tell you who now heads the Chrysler Corporation or a food producer like Hormel.

Bill Gates is a special case. He is probably the most famous company head in the world today, but he doesn't have the kind of outgoing, flamboyant personality associated with a Turner, Iacocca, or Purdue. Although he is capable of giving a speech at a computer convention that has people in the industry hanging on every word, he doesn't achieve that end because of any particular oratorical or theatrical gift. He is very articulate, but his voice is somewhat high-pitched, and he is far from having a charismatic presence. He does have a sense of humor and a winning, rather boyish smile, which he uses to good effect when being interviewed by someone like David Frost, famous for his lengthy Nixon interviews. In both print and television interviews, Gates demonstrates a talent for ex-

I make it a point to read at least one newsweekly from cover to cover because it broadens my interests. If I read only what intrigues me, such as the science section and a subset of the business section, then I finish the magazine the same person I was before I started. So I read it all.

—BILL GATES, 1995

plaining complicated ideas simply and clearly, making excellent use of anecdotes and references to well-known realities to explore the meaning of the emerging electronic world. But there is seldom the sense of someone giving a performance that marks a man like Lee Iacocca or Donald Trump. Bill Gates gets listened to chiefly because what he has to say is interesting and important.

For the general public, of course, there is another factor that goes beyond the fact that he is one of the primary leaders in changing the way the world works and plays: he is the richest man on the planet. Even a year or two ago there were a couple of Arab oil sheiks who were considered to be richer, but no longer. For the last two years, since the launch of Windows 95, Gates's worth has been increasing by tens of millions of dollars a day, on average, with his total worth now estimated to be in excess of $35 billion. This is, of course, his worth on paper, since it is tied to his twenty-five percent share of Microsoft stock. If the stock goes down, so does his worth. No one knows what his cash worth is, and he's not about to announce it.

As moguls go, however, Bill Gates is not particularly secretive. He has always been willing to talk about his youth at the Lakeside School and Harvard, focusing on his discovery of the world of computers with his friend Paul Allen, but including stories about acting in Peter Shaffer's *Black Comedy* at Lakeside and playing marathon poker games in the dormitory at Harvard. He doesn't mind people knowing that he and Allen lived for a long time mainly on Cokes and pizza, or that he slept under his desk on many occasions. There are those who have known him who say that, at least until recently, Gates was something of an overgrown boy, however rich and brilliant, and perhaps his willingness to talk about his youthful antics is in part

I used to work all night in the office, but it's been quite a while since I lived on catnaps. I like to get seven hours of sleep a night because that's what I need to stay sharp and creative and upbeat.

—BILL GATES, 1996

a reflection of that. But many others find that aspect of him considerably more charming than the pretense on the part of many important people that they never had an adolescence.

Much has been made in the press of a certain physical sloppiness on the part of Gates, with references to perpetually smudged eyeglasses, a lack of attention to his wardrobe, and (in tones of coy horror) a disinclination to bathe as often as he might. But although he is clearly far from a fashion plate, he seems to have paid more attention to his physical appearance in recent years, and when giving speeches or making television appearances he is decently enough turned out. The press has also been fixated on his habits of rocking back and forth from the waist up when thinking or incessantly tapping his feet. On television interviews, there is some evidence of restless legs but very little in the way of rocking; instead there tends to be an upper body stiffness that suggests he is consciously controlling that tendency. It has been noted that his father has a habit of rocking, too, but in a much less pronounced way.

Interestingly, despite the media's emphasis on Gates's "geekiness," some reporters have also suggested that in the past he has been something of a ladies' man. The contradiction in terms is amusing, and below the surface what the press really seems to have been talking about was Gates's unwillingness to get deeply involved with one woman during the period he was building Microsoft into a software empire. Whether it was his unwillingness or the fact that a man given to putting in eighteen-hour workdays is something less than a romantic ideal remains an open question.

According to many reports, he was involved in the early 1980s with a Seattle computer equipment salesperson

Why do I work hard rather than retire? The answer is simple: I do what I find interesting and challenging, and I think I have the best job in the world. Most people struggle on one level or another for economic security. What would they do once they had it? Would they play tennis all day? Would they read books? I like recreation and I love to read books, but the most enjoyable challenges come from work. I am nowhere near retiring.

—Bill Gates, 1995

named Jill Bennett, who is quoted by James Wallace in *Overdrive* as saying, "Although he hides it well with his hard-core exterior, and certainly will not admit it, Bill's feelings get hurt easily." But Gates didn't have much time for a serious relationship. He then took up with Ann Winblad, who built a software company from scratch in Minneapolis and then sold it for millions. They apparently had a great deal in common, although Winblad was five years older. Gates still wasn't interested in marriage, and they broke up not long after he first met Melinda French in 1987. French had recently started working for Microsoft; she was nine years younger than Gates.

The relationship with Melinda French developed gradually, with a few on-again off-again patches, into the early 1990s, when Gates, according to various friends, began to indicate that he was seriously in love with her. It is known that both his parents, and especially his mother, Mary, were pushing Gates to get married. Several male friends who were already married and had children have said that Gates talked with them about what it means to be married when one's work plays such a central place in one's life. Many people who know Gates well have said that Melinda French was an exceptionally good match for him. Not only did she know the computer business well enough to keep up with his intellectual and business interests but perhaps even more important, she was also a strong, independent woman with interests of her own, who was already serving on the board of a Seattle theater company. She was, in that regard, like Bill Gates's mother, a woman perfectly capable of occupying her own time in fruitful, even important, ways.

Although Gates had broken off romantically with Ann Winblad years earlier, they had remained extremely close

I can't be neutral or dispassionate about Warren Buffett, because we're close friends. We recently vacationed together in China with our wives. I think his jokes are all funny. I think his dietary practices—lots of burgers and Cokes—are excellent. In short, I'm a fan.

—BILL GATES, issuing a disclaimer at the start of a review of Roger Lowenstein's biography of Gates's fellow billionaire, for *Fortune,* 1996

friends, and Bill Gates revealed to *Time* that he had consulted with Winblad before proposing to Melinda French. Winblad approved. And as if demonstrating her own strength and independence, Melinda French agreed that Gates could go on spending a week each year with Winblad at her cottage on North Carolina's Outer Banks. This long-standing excursion is described by both Gates and Winblad as a chance to unwind and talk about the world. That this yearly rendezvous is so openly acknowledged lends credence to the idea that it is also completely aboveboard. What Melinda French Gates really thinks about it, however, is unknown; she does not give interviews, although she apparently has no problem with her husband's discussing such subjects as the raising of their children when he is asked questions in interviews.

Both Gates and his good friend and fellow billionaire Warren Buffett have talked about how Gates proposed to French. Gates and French were returning from Palm Springs on a chartered jet, which Gates arranged to have land in Omaha, Nebraska. The reason was that Buffett owned a jewelry store there, and even though it was a Sunday night, he personally opened it up and helped the couple pick out an engagement ring. For a supposed "computer nerd," this sounds more like a romantic plotline out of a Danielle Steel novel.

The proposal, and the bestowal of an engagement ring with an enormous diamond, took place on the final weekend of March in 1993. The bride-to-be was not just an anonymous Microsoft employee. Since being recruited in 1987, she had risen steadily through the middle-management ranks and was now a unit manager for the desktop publishing software known as Microsoft Publisher, in charge of nearly fifty employees. With her stock options, she had

A relationship with Bill early on is a test. Are you smart enough? Do you have enough common sense? Can you make the grade? Are you athletic enough? Melinda is Bill's pick. He could have chosen any woman as a wife for life. He has chosen her, and that means she is an exceptional woman.

—ANN WINBLAD, quoted in *Overdrive*, 1997

become one of the twenty-five hundred Microsoft million-aires. During the engagement she went right on working, but it had been decided that she would not continue after the marriage. Although there was inevitably a great deal of press coverage when the engagement was announced two days after the special trip to Omaha—word had already spread through Microsoft in a deluge of e-mail—her friends and family followed her wishes and refused to give interviews. Even former neighbors in Seattle and in Dallas, where she had grown up, were asked to keep quiet, and with security considerations having been made explicit, almost all complied. The few people who were willing to talk to reporters were mostly friends of Bill Gates, and they universally touted the match as an excellent one.

The wedding took place nine months later on January 1, 1994, on the Hawaiian island of Lanai. Lanai is small, largely covered with former pineapple fields. It has only three thousand permanent residents, and its two plush, secluded resorts, built in 1990 and 1991, are favored by Hollywood stars who cherish their privacy. Gates rented all the rooms at both hotels, for security reasons, although many were not needed for the fewer than one hundred fifty guests. They included a number of Microsoft executives, headed by Steve Ballmer, who was best man, Paul Allen, close friends like Warren Buffett and former girlfriend Ann Winblad, and a single media luminary, *Washington Post* owner Katherine Graham, who was a longtime friend of the Gates family. Great effort had been taken to keep the wedding secret from the press, and although word leaked out in the last day or two before the wedding, the island was too cut off for the media to mount a paparazzi assault.

Most of the guests arrived several days before the Sat-

Evolution is many orders of magnitude ahead of mankind today in creating a complex system. I don't think it's irreconcilable to say we will understand the human mind someday and explain it in software-like terms, and also to say it is a creation that shouldn't be compared to software. Religion has come around to the view that even things that can be explained scientifically can have an underlying purpose that goes beyond the science. Even though I am not religious, the amazement and wonder I have about the human mind is closer to religious awe than dispassionate analysis.

—BILL GATES, to *Time*, 1997

urday of the ceremony. They were able to play golf on the island's two courses, one designed by Jack Nicklaus, the other by Greg Norman. There were parties, gifts for the guests every day, a luau with fireworks. On New Year's Eve, Bill Gates sprung a very special surprise on Melinda French as he casually introduced her favorite singer, Willie Nelson, who performed on the private beach of the Manele Bay Hotel where the Gates and French families were staying. According to James Wallace, the highlight of the evening came when Nelson sang, "I've got the money, honey, if you've got the time."

Paul Allen had had his yacht sailed to Hawaii and hosted a champagne brunch aboard it on the wedding day. Guests were driven out to the twelfth tee of the Manele Bay Hotel in golf carts in the late afternoon. There, on a spectacular cliff-side site, the ceremony was performed by Father William Sullivan, the president of Seattle University. French is Catholic, and it has been reported that the couple's children will be raised as Catholics unless Bill Gates should commit himself fully to some other religion. That seems doubtful since, as he explained to David Frost, he tends to look for scientific explanations for things, much as he says he respects the moral principles of the major religions.

It seems likely that the happiest person at the wedding, aside from the bride and groom, was Mary Gates. She was very seriously ill with cancer, and there had even been concern that she would not be well enough to attend her son's wedding. Friends of the family have said that her fortitude in being there was a remarkable demonstration of human will and inner strength. Shortly after returning home, she became so ill that the remaining months of her

I am the son of Mary Gates, and she was a wonderful woman. Not many adult sons are as proud of their mother as I was.

—BILL GATES, at his mother's funeral, 1994

life were spent largely in seclusion. She was only sixty-four when she died in her sleep in June 1994.

Bill and Melinda Gates took up residence in the home he had bought a few months earlier less than a mile from the $40 million house he had begun building on a bluff over Lake Washington in 1993. This dream house has been much talked and written about, but it was to undergo further changes requested by Melinda Gates. From the start it had been designed with a future family in mind, having a children's wing and live-in facilities for a nanny. The high-tech aspects of the house have received particular attention. It has been wired beyond most people's imagination, with the capacity to give Gates and his family, or any guest, an enormous variety of music in the air or art on the walls according to the whim of the moment. There were those who speculated that Melinda French Gates was insisting upon cutting back on the technology, but more recent reports suggest that her main concern was what she saw as an excess of exposed concrete. Gates himself, it turns out, saw the importance of making sure that the house had warmth as well as futuristic technical wonders, and he was extremely conscious of the kind of detailing that would achieve that end. Despite its size, photographs of the unfinished structure have revealed an architectural conception, including recycled Douglas fir beams, that is not at all out of place on Lake Washington. In the spring of 1997, Bill and Melinda Gates hosted the first large-scale dinner at the still unfinished house as part of a Microsoft "C.E.O. Summit" attended by heavy hitters from twenty-five countries, not to mention Vice President Al Gore, Steve Forbes, and the chairman of the Federal Communications Commission, Reed E. Hundt. The *New York Times* noted that one guest, Paul Hazen of Wells Fargo & Company,

When you visit, you'll get an electronic pin encoded with your preferences. As you wander toward any room, your favorite pictures will appear, along with music you like or a TV show or movie you're watching. The system will learn from your choices, and it will remember the music or pictures from your previous visits so you can choose to have them again or have similar but new ones. We'll have to have hierarchy guidelines, for when more than one person goes to a room.

—BILL GATES, to *Time,* 1997

passed the word that the house "is so full of beautiful wood and detail that those touches seemed to upstage high-tech features like the huge video screen that took up a full wall in the dining room."

Several of Gates's main rivals in the computer software business expressed hope at the time of his marriage that it would change his workaholic habits and slow him down a bit. But in fact he had already slowed down some, without in any way becoming less aggressive as a businessman. There had been a time, as he told David Frost, when he had gone for nearly three days without sleep when working on an urgent problem, but he hadn't done that in some time. As he got older, he found that he needed a good seven hours' sleep in order to be as sharp as he needed to be. In a number of interviews, he made it clear that the advent of e-mail made his life easier to manage—it was now possible, for example, to work intermittently at home over the weekends, dispatching necessary instructions, notes, or ideas electronically. He still puts in what many would consider prodigious working hours, often twelve a day at the office or on his many business trips, and six to eight hours at home on weekends. A telling comment on the subject of religion was his assertion to *Time* that "just in terms of allocation of resources, religion is not very efficient. There's a lot more I could be doing on a Sunday morning."

But it is clear that even though he is still driven by ambition and a vision of the future that he is determined to make real, he is more capable of taking a break than many would have thought possible a few years ago. His visit to China in September of 1995 is a case in point. In March of 1994, Gates had gone to China on business, a difficult and confrontational visit in which he had been given a rough time by the Chinese Ministry of Electronics

I'd like to understand how the human brain works. If there was an ultimate answer machine, that's the question I'd ask. I'm in awe of the brain and its ability to learn. I'm fascinated by such things as how a child picks up languages, by mental disorders such as autism, and by the role of the limbic brain in letting aromas trigger mood changes. I really enjoy reading about the brain, the secrets of which are among the great mysteries of science.

—BILL GATES, 1997

Industry, whose officials had been upset that the Chinese version of Windows 3.1 had been developed on Taiwan instead of in cooperation with the mainland China computer industry. The software also did not use the simplified Chinese pictographs introduced by the Communist government in the 1950s to combat widespread illiteracy; rather they featured the traditional characters still in use on Taiwan and in Hong Kong. China's president Jiang Zemin, according to James Wallace, bluntly told Gates he had much to learn abut the "five thousand years of Chinese history." In the next several months, Gates had to restructure his entire approach to China in order to win government endorsement of Windows 95. His return to China in September of 1995 was not a business trip but a vacation, with the added benefit of a chance to learn more about the country. Gates boasted to David Frost that he had not even taken his computer with him or contacted Microsoft during the two-week vacation. He and his wife, along with the Buffetts and several other couples, instead went sightseeing—and played a lot of bridge. With Windows 95 successfully launched the previous month and antitrust actions by the U.S. government beaten back for the time being, he could afford to take some time off. According to many reports, he needed to do so, with several commentators suggesting that he was as close to exhaustion as he had ever come.

Melinda Gates was already pregnant during the trip to China, and on April 26, 1996, she gave birth to their daughter, Jennifer Katherine Gates. Many Gates watchers, and even his friends, wondered what kind of father he would make. That question was answered sooner than expected. He told several interviewers that he hadn't expected to have that much interest in a child until he or she learned

My kids will have computers, of course. But they'll have books first.

—BILL GATES, 1996

to talk, but that Jennifer had proved "much more of a thrill than I expected," as he told the *New York Times.* To *Time* in January 1997 he admitted, " . . . I'm totally into it now. She's just started to say 'ba-ba' and have a personality."

Even before Jennifer was born, Bill Gates made it clear that he had thought a lot about how to bring up children. Because of who he is, he recognized that there would be problems about his children being approached differently than other kids, and security problems would always have to be taken into consideration. The security issue was not a new one, however. There had been an attempt to kidnap his mother as far back as 1984, according to James Wallace. But in talking to David Frost, Gates emphasized what he had learned from his own parents about raising kids, praising them for their willingness to listen to their children and to take their opinions seriously from a fairly young age. He noted that his parents had encouraged "sharing problems in a way that made them interesting to think about them, not to worry about them, but to consider all the possibilities." He also made a point, as he often does, about his parents setting an example by reading a great deal.

Bill Gates has gone on record many times as saying that he does not plan to leave his children vast fortunes, and has even said that $10 million each seemed like more than enough. To most people that sounds like an enormous amount of money, but considering Gates's $35 billion fortune, it could almost be considered paltry. The great bulk of his fortune, Gates insists, will be given away. There have been some critics who have suggested that he was not moving fast enough on the charitable front, but by early 1996, he had given more then $60 million to several univer-

Warren [Buffett] and I share certain values. We both feel lucky that we were born into an era in which our skills have turned out to be so remunerative. Had we been born at a different time, our skills might not have had much value. Since we don't plan on spending much of what we have accumulated, we can make sure our wealth benefits society. In a sense, we're both working for charity. In any case, our heirs will get only a small portion of what we accumulate, because we both believe that passing on huge wealth to children isn't in their or society's interest. Warren likes to say that he wants to give his children enough money for them to do anything, but not enough for them to do nothing. I thought about this before I met Warren, and hearing him articulate it crystallized my feelings.

—BILL GATES, 1996

sities, and established a $200 million foundation administered by his father. Several more significant gifts were made in 1997, topped by the $400 million gift to public libraries, particularly in the inner cities, for computers and computer software, with half the money coming from his personal fortune and half from Microsoft in the form of actual software. Gates has said that he intends to focus on running Microsoft for another ten years and then to turn his attention more and more to the process of giving his money away. While some of America's great philanthropists of the past, such as John D. Rockefeller and Andrew Carnegie, seemed to turn to philanthropy in part to clear their names of charges that they had ruthlessly exploited their workers and gouged the public, Gates has for many years talked about the importance of giving back a great deal to the society that fostered his success. For all the accusations of monopolistic practices brought by competitors, Gates's reputation has never been besmirched in the ways Rockefeller's and Carnegie's were. His mother's many years of devotion to The United Way and other charities appear to have planted a philanthropic seed from the start.

Bill Gates the businessman is often feared and sometimes reviled, most often by other computer industry leaders whom he has bested, but Bill Gates the man seems determined to see to it that he is remembered not just as a computer genius, or the one-time richest man in the world, or even as one of the most important shapers of a new age of electronic information, but also as someone who helped make the world a better place. Only future generations can arrive at a final estimation of the ways in which Bill Gates changed the world for better or worse, but he is clearly aware that his legacy will be judged on

I am offered countless opportunities to invest or make charitable contributions, gifts, or loans. Some people want a few hundred dollars, some a few hundred million. . . . Spending money intelligently is as difficult as earning it. Giving away money in meaningful ways will be a main preoccupation later in my life, assuming I still have a lot to give away.

—BILL GATES, 1995

the basis of the entire spectrum of his endeavors. Bill Gates admires other people who have a "wide bandwidth," and he seems determined to live his life in a way that demonstrates that he has that quality also.

CHAPTER EIGHT

―――――――――

A VISION OF THE FUTURE

Well, twenty years ago, when we started, we talked about a computer on every desk and in every home. Now, if you take that to its extreme and say one hundred percent of the people, clearly we'll never get there. There'll always be some people who choose not to participate, just like some people don't use the phone or watch TV.

—BILL GATES responds to a question about people who don't use computers, 1995

All companies, whether they make games, like Parker Brothers, or cereals, like General Mills, must think about the future, about new products and new ways of marketing them. But in the world of computer hardware and software, thinking about the future is the name of the game. That well-worn phrase "The future is now" isn't good enough. Unless computer companies constantly press the boundaries of the possible, they will find themselves suddenly looking up to discover that "the future was yesterday," because some other more innovative company has gotten ahead of them.

Bill Gates, as much as anyone else on the planet, has had his eye firmly fixed on the future since he was barely a teenager. It is precisely because he has always thought about not merely what comes next but what comes after "next" that his company dominates the software market around the world. But while technological development is his business, he has given far more thought to the implications—not only for businesses but also for individuals and for society as a whole—of the changes that new computer technology will bring. As he has noted, computers have changed the world more quickly than any other technology man has ever created. New technologies, from the repeating rifle to the steam engine, from the combustion engine to electricity, have always taken time to really take hold. The atomic bomb, because of its power to destroy the world, had a vast immediate effect on the way both individuals and nations thought about the world, but its power to destroy has kept it from being used, and its peaceful offshoot, atomic energy, has had a very mixed history. Because no other technology has developed so quickly—doubling yearly in capacity even as it came down in cost, according to Moore's Law—computer technology,

Computers will become truly intelligent someday—but I question whether this will happen in
my lifetime. On the other hand, computers are on
the verge of being able to talk, and when they do
it will be easy to imagine that they are intelligent.
Within a few years even small, affordable personal
computers might have personalities and possibly
idiosyncrasies. These machines will speak in a
rather natural human voice, if that's what we
want. . . . giving computers the trappings of intelli-
gence will make them easier to use. But it won't
mean they really think—yet.

—BILL GATES, 1995

and particularly its manifestation in the PC revolution, has changed the way a greater number of people live more quickly than anything that has gone before.

Computer development continues at such a fast pace that even someone as obsessed with its course as Bill Gates almost missed the importance of the Internet. However, because of the enormous resources of his company and his own ability to shift gears, he was able to succeed at playing catch-up in a way that many major computer companies failed to do. He is fully aware that next time he and Microsoft might not be so fortunate; the experience with the Internet has only redoubled his focus on the future. Over the past few years no one in the computer business, and even few of those academic or think-tank individuals known as "futurists," have spoken out with more frequency and force about where we are headed. We live in a very complex time, in which technological and social change, each affecting the other both positively and negatively, occur with almost dizzying speed, and it is possible that even Bill Gates will miss seeing a crucial turn in the road (though not for lack of attention). His view of the future is both broad enough and complex enough to be of importance even if he does not have enough power to actually shape its course.

Gates has said innumerable times that he is an optimist and that he believes the future computers help create will be for the general betterment of humankind. But he is not blind to the dislocations that will occur. He has noted that no great change is ever completely for the best. By way of example, he points out that while the telephone made it possible for people to reach out and remain closer to people at a distance, it may also have led to a lessening of closeness within the neighborhood. And the "razzle-daz-

Voting is an important example of an information activity that could be improved with the help of the Internet. Where I live, we vote for judges, but I often don't know who deserves my ballot because little information about their judicial records is readily available. I look forward to an Internet-based alternative. Instead of voting in person or mailing in an absentee ballot, I expect to be able to vote from my PC.

—Bill Gates, 1996

zle" of television, he admits, makes it more difficult for teachers to command the attention of students in school. But while computers may seem likely to accentuate both these problems, Gates holds out the hope that the rise of the Internet and the eventual creation of a true information highway, which is only in its early stages, may well succeed in countering—even reversing—these effects.

The ability of the Internet and the World Wide Web to transcend national boundaries, he believes, will promote a far greater understanding between the peoples of different cultures, and that understanding, as he sees it, cannot help but make for a more peaceful and less fractious world. This is an optimistic, even idealistic, view. There are those who would point to the Middle East, Northern Ireland, and the fragments of Yugoslavia and suggest that familiarity seems only to breed contempt. But Gates takes a larger view, suggesting that the nature of the World Wide Web can transcend what are in many cases localized enmities.

He does not believe, however, that the Internet will remain the wild and wooly entity that now exists. Gates treads a fine line on this issue. He notes that because the world has never before had a global medium that makes it possible for anyone to "publish" his or her views, it is sometimes difficult to determine who should be held accountable when material that some deem to be offensive is published on the World Wide Web. Gates recognizes that the issue of accountability is going to be difficult to settle, because different countries have a variety of views on what is libelous or offensive, and differing laws on matters of accountability. His views on the tricky nature of this problem have been borne out by actions taken in Germany, which has made neo-Nazi propaganda illegal on the Internet and takes the view that the companies acting as tech-

Some people think the Internet should be wide open. They believe interactive networks are a world apart in which copyright, libel, pornography, and confidentiality laws do not apply. This is a naive dream, which fails to recognize that the Internet is going to be a vital part of mainstream life, not a lawless backwater.

At the other extreme, some people think the Internet should be tightly controlled. They would ruin the Internet in the name of reining it in.

—Bill Gates, 1996

nological facilitators—say, Compuserve or America Online—are legally responsible for the content that is accessible through their services.

But while recognizing the importance of accountability, Gates is concerned about governments' restricting what can be on the Internet to the extent that they undermine the free flow of information, which is its most important characteristic. In 1996, he took immediate steps to make clear his opposition to the Communications Decency Act, a part of the Telecommunications Reform Act passed by the U.S. Congress, because it made it a felony to publish on the Internet "detailed information about birth control, AIDS prevention and how to get a legal abortion." In July of 1997, the Supreme Court made clear that it was on the side of Gates and other Internet advocates in striking down the Communications Decency Act as unconstitutional, firmly stating that the Internet could not be regulated in the way that television and radio are. This was the first major case in which the Supreme Court dealt with what promises to be a long string of laws on Internet communications over the next decade.

On the other hand, Gates does not believe that the Internet can be a wide-open medium in which any kind of material is available to anyone. He is concerned about the possibility of children stumbling onto pornographic material, of course, but he also notes that the Internet is now the repository of misinformation, outright lies, and disturbing propaganda that can also be dangerous to children and adults. He has had considerable personal experience with anonymous Internet users pretending to be him. These "impostors sometimes do incredibly nasty things, such as sending electronic mail in my name that promises people jobs or money or criticizes Apple Macintosh." And al-

Eventually I expect that anyone publishing information on a network will be expected to catego-
rize it in an agreed upon way, to indicate its nature.
The software used to access the Internet or commercial electronic communities will filter information based on how it is categorized. Software for
use by children will reject adult-oriented content,
for example. In order for self-categorization to be
effective, the sources of information on a network
must be authenticated so that people and companies can be held accountable for the information
they distribute electronically.

—BILL GATES, 1995

though Gates has not brought it up, there are Web sites that can only be described as "Bill Gates hate forums."

Gates thinks that the problems of offensive material on the Internet can be dealt with through a combination of technology and industry self-government without trying to make the Internet absurdly bland. He suggests that "authorized organizations" should develop a ratings system for Web pages, making it possible for software to block material that people do not want their children to have access to or that they themselves do not want to receive. Microsoft itself, as well as many other companies, began building ratings capabilities into software in 1996, and Internet services have been moving to provide parents with blocking agents.

While granting that no ratings system can attain perfection—people's ideas of acceptability vary too widely for that—Gates believes that systems will be devised that will satisfy the great majority of people. He even thinks it will be feasible to keep a compartmentalized area of the Internet functioning in the anonymous chat room format that currently appeals to many users. Because that area would be compartmentalized, users would know that they were getting into a fairly anarchic situation; those who desired to do so could, while those who wanted to stay away from such free-form communication would know to avoid it or block it from children.

Although Bill Gates recognizes the necessity of dealing with these problems, understanding that many of them will be difficult to settle, he is obviously far happier touting the extraordinary benefits he is convinced the Internet can bring. While he may have been a little slow in recognizing the importance of the Internet, no one has subsequently been a more enthusiastic promoter of its potential. Gates

The most important use of information technology today is to improve education, and we have a tremendous opportunity to enhance the ways we think and learn by taking advantage of the computer as a learning tool. Microsoft envisions using technology to create a "Connected Learning Community," in which all students have access to the world's information through personal computers, and students, educators, parents, and the extended community are connected to each other.

—BILL GATES, 1996

has focused especially on the educational aspects of the Internet, and he is clearly certain that it not only can but will help provide greater educational opportunities to more people, both children and adults, than has ever before been possible.

Gates has dealt with the issues of computers and education in numerous forums. He has devoted several of his newspaper columns to it, has answered questions about his views in many television and newspaper interviews, and has even appeared on a Nickelodeon news special with Linda Ellerbee, where he answered questions posed by a group of young children, some familiar with computers and some not. A chapter of *The Road Ahead*, called "Education: The Best Investment," deals with the subject in detail. Not only has Gates done his homework on this complex issue but he also clearly has a genuine interest in it. His views are far more substantial than the usual politically correct fluff one gets from business leaders trying to score brownie points to demonstrate their civic virtue.

Gates doesn't try to dodge or cover over the problems that stand in the way of making electronic education work. He admits up front in *The Road Ahead*, for example, that so far educational technology has been "overhyped and has failed to deliver on its promises." He is fully aware of the conservatism in the educational establishment that, combined with the anxieties of older teachers, creates resistance to new technologies. He recognizes the acute funding problems that beset education, particularly in urban and rural locales.

On the other side of the coin, Gates emphasizes the importance of good teachers and the need that children have for social interaction with other children and adults in a school setting. He points out that pilot programs using

Among all the types of paper documents, narrative fiction is one of the few that will not benefit from electronic organization. Almost every reference book has an index, but novels don't because there isn't a need to be able to look something up in a novel. Novels are linear. Likewise, we'll continue to watch most movies from start to finish. This isn't a technological judgment—it is an artistic one. Their linearity is intrinsic to the storytelling process.

—BILL GATES, 1995

computer technology demonstrate that the students do best and are happiest when there is a teacher readily available to assist, answer questions, and encourage them. He sees the eventual development of an information highway that gives both students and teachers vastly increased access to information that can be used by both to give greater depth and meaning to education. Yes, students will get to interact with their computers, but that experience will serve as a basis for greater interaction between the individual teacher and student on a person-to-person basis. There are those who envision a future in which classrooms barely exist, students doing almost all their learning at home in front of a computer. Some believe this is what ought to happen; others hold up this vision as a warning against a dehumanization of the entire educational process. Bill Gates, on the contrary, sees the information highway and universal access to computer technology as a means of enriching an educational environment in which the interaction between student and teacher still plays a crucial role.

The depth and variety of information available in such a setting will, however, make it possible for the teacher to customize the rate and nature of the learning experience more directly to the individual student. Different speeds of learning will thus be more easily accommodated within the same classroom, and students with particular gifts and interests will be able to explore those also. Gates doesn't just hypothesize about the potential benefits of new technology; he reports on pilot programs that have met with success in specific schools, some of them particularly troubled ones. The media tend to emphasize Bill Gates's technical genius, business acumen, and vast wealth, but one of the things that makes him unusual in the world of high technology is a surprising appreciation of the human need

Even with all this global knowledge available, computers will never become substitutes for great teachers. In fact, using computers in the learning process is effective only when teachers are involved. Computers only can be relied upon to impart some of the knowledge—we need teachers' expertise to integrate technology into daily lessons, to become facilitators and coaches, which will enable them to spend more time one-on-one with students.

—BILL GATES in *THE Journal* (Technological Horizons in Education), 1996

for personal mentors. He singles out a chemistry teacher who brought the subject alive for him, and he has noted again and again how much of a stimulus his friendship with Paul Allen was right from the start. He appreciates the importance of personality and individuality, and his views on the future of education make it abundantly clear that he is not the kind of "loner" his stereotype as a computer whiz would have him be.

In July of 1997, Gates put his money where his mouth is in terms of education by setting up a foundation to spend $200 million of his own fortune on computers for public libraries, backed up by an additional $200 million in software from Microsoft. The press (which had been asking for some time what Gates intended to do with his billions in terms of charity) quickly compared this gift to the building of more than twenty-eight hundred public libraries by the steel magnate Andrew Carnegie early in the century. Most public comment on Gates's gift was laudatory, but there was the usual sprinkling of negative reaction that greets even the charitable efforts of the very rich. Some commentators suggested that the money could have been better spent on books and noted that Gates would at least indirectly profit from the further dissemination of Microsoft products in a way that had not been true of Carnegie. One letter to the *New York Times* went so far as to suggest that the gift, with its emphasis on inner-city libraries, was simply a way of creating a generation of low-paid computer drones by giving poor children just enough training to make them suitable for future exploitation. Such attacks seemed intent upon ignoring Gates's long-held belief that the future of education depends upon giving every child a chance to participate in the gradual development of the information highway.

In many neighborhoods, such as the one I grew up in, almost everybody frequents the library. About half of the U.S. population uses one or more of the country's sixteen thousand library branches, which are twice as numerous as Mc-Donald's restaurants, a statistic that surprised me.

Libraries are a smart way to subsidize public access to information, because the investment benefits a community of people—and on a completely evenhanded basis, with no stigma attached. No one says to somebody who uses a library, "Oh, you can't afford your own books."

—BILL GATES, a year before his $400 million gift to public libraries,
1996

Bill Gates's broader vision of the future does, however, require an American public—and, eventually, a world population—for whom the use of computers is second nature. And such a world will without doubt enrich the coffers of Microsoft and every other successful software and hardware computer company. One of his pet ideas is the development of what he calls a Wallet PC. This extraordinary piece of miniaturized computer hardware would not be much bigger than the wallets we now carry in our pockets, but it would have a variety of uses that even science fiction writers might have regarded as a stretch in the 1970s. It would serve as identification, notebook, and engagement calendar. It would contain electronic signals that would take the place of door and car keys, and pictures of one's family or latest vacation trip could be called up on its small screen. Most important, it would usher in the "cashless society" that so many computer visionaries have long imagined. It would work for all purchases, even vending machines, with any transaction immediately transmitted to one's central banking or credit account. The Wallet PC would even be capable of transferring money to your children's Wallet PC when a kid says, "Dad, can I have ten bucks?"

Banks are already issuing "smart cards" and "check cards" that allow many purchases to be paid for directly out of one's bank account, bypassing credit cards, but some retailers, according to newspaper accounts, are starting to balk at the charges that banks are levying on them. If this heats up into a real revolt and the consumer ends up paying the costs of such transactions, it may spell trouble for the supposedly imminent cashless society. What's more, computers are not yet ready to handle the incredible load of financial information that would have to be processed

As bankers contemplate updating their systems and products to reflect the opportunities presented by the Internet, they should recognize that simply converting products to the on-line world, with little value added, will inevitably lead to competition based on little other than price. To differentiate its on-line products, a bank must add value—and continually refine its offerings. The inertia which today means customers seldom consider moving their business is no longer a factor in an on-line environment. Mobility is just a few keystrokes away. Future customer loyalty will be hard-earned.

—Bill Gates, 1996

in a world in which even a single purchase of a fifty cent candybar would have to be transmitted instantly to financial institutions. Gates, however, is not deterred by these logistical problems, which he believes technology can overcome, although he has admitted that some people will refuse to use Wallet PCs, just as some people refuse to have phones or television sets even now. Given the millions of Americans who do not even have bank accounts, the resistance may be greater than Gates is counting on.

Still, Bill Gates is far from the most wild-eyed futurist around. There are those who claim that a cashless society, for example, will totally eradicate the so-called underground economy that is the theater of operations for everyone from drug dealers and car thieves to petty burglars, not to mention quite a few politicians over the years. These utopian forecasters are ignoring a problem that Gates himself is fully aware of and quite worried about: computerized theft. It has been said that many famous bank robbers, including the legendary Willie Sutton, were quite smart enough to be bank presidents, but found robbery easier and more exciting. Over the past twenty years, the number of criminals specializing in computer crime has risen just as fast as computer usage. In the last year, the media have focused for the first time on the growing number of people whose complete identities have been stolen electronically—their Social Security and driver's license numbers, along with credit card information. These people have not lost their wallets: their identities have been swiped even as they engaged in legitimate commercial transactions that were carried out by computer. They have suddenly discovered that their credit is ruined and that they are liable for astronomical bills. It can take months of work to prove that they

It always takes time for these things to happen, so how long will it be before there's no vending machine that takes coins and things? Probably twenty years or more, but the convenience of not having to carry coins around and being able to just debit the right amount, it's pretty darn attractive, and in fact it's less expensive to build a vending machine that does this electronic communication than one that tries to recognize fake coins and have people come around to collect it physically.

—BILL GATES on the Wallet PC and the cashless society, 1995

are who they say they are and that someone has purloined their lives.

Bill Gates recognizes the problems in this area, but, once again, he believes that they can be solved with new technology. He has stated that the Wallet PC will in fact be better protected than today's wallet because it will be possible to deactivate the entire device at once if it is stolen, rather than having to contact a number of separate institutions to report missing credit cards, checks, and identification. And he notes that security codes are one of the most important if least talked-about areas of computer research.

Security codes are crucial not only to safeguarding financial transactions but also to the question of privacy. Gates has written and spoken about the privacy issue on numerous occasions. "Steaming open an envelope," he has said, "has never been so simple and untraceable as it is, in effect, on the Internet." He sees some technological solutions to the problem, making it impossible, for example, for e-mail to be forwarded or even printed out, or ensuring that it can't be read more than once, when it first appears on the recipient's screen. But he admits that technology can't solve all privacy problems. The media have recently been focusing on the fact that most people have no idea how much information on their lives is gathered by computer, or that that information is routinely sold to other companies looking to extend their lists of consumers for marketing purposes. For example, when people use the cards issued by supermarket chains to get an automatic lower price on specials, that information is recorded and can be resold to marketing companies that want to know exactly what soap powders and cereals you buy. Gates was dealing with this issue two years ago, long before the media got interested.

If you're worried about threats to privacy in the emerging electronic age, you're not alone. I'm worried, too. "Information at your fingertips," a Microsoft motto, is the promise of the electronic age. But we need to be careful about what information and at whose fingertips.

—BILL GATES, 1995

In Gates's view, the privacy issue is one that will have to be dealt with as a matter of public policy, by governments around the world. He notes that there are already many privacy laws on the books, and that these will have to be extended to deal with the electronic community of the information age. But he cautions against rushing into the passing of such laws, believing that a major public debate must take place first.

Finally, there is a major area of future computer development that Gates is preoccupied with as much for business reasons as for any broader vision he has of twenty-first-century life. That involves the conjunction of computers and television. What Gates and many other computer business leaders want to see is television sets capable of a clarity that makes it possible for them to carry not only the coming HDTV picture emanating from broadcast channels, already mandated by Congress, but also the textual material so important to Internet and PC usage. He wants to see broadcast television and PC screens merge into a single unit. But the makers of television sets and the major television networks and cable companies do not want to move in that direction, chiefly because the new HDTV sets are going to be expensive enough to begin with without adding to their cost by making them compatible with PCs. The television people simply do not believe that every household is going to have a PC, and that even if PC usage grows faster than they expect, the public really doesn't want a merger of the two mediums, but would rather have separate appliances for separate uses.

One of the issues being contested here rests on the fact that PCs are still far too complicated to use to be considered appliances in the way that television sets are. You can't just push a button with a PC as you can with a televi-

Tomorrow's communications systems will let you decide who can reach you in the morning, who can reach you at the dinner hour, and who can reach you at midnight. You'll set the rules. You'll decide that a certain salesperson can call you back only once, or only between certain hours, or that particular people should be allowed to leave voice or e-mail messages while others should not.

—BILL GATES, 1997

sion set. The television industries have taken note that while recent polls have shown the VCR to be the American public's favorite appliance, the majority of owners do not know how to program them to record programs off the air. VCRs are used simply to play rented or purchased videotapes. PCs are vastly more complicated to use than VCRs, and the television industry believes it will be a long time before enough people buy and learn how to use PCs as they currently work, or before something simple enough to be considered an appliance replaces them, to make the fusion of television and PCs a good marketing bet. Harsh words have been traded on this issue, with Gates and some other computer company CEOs saying that the television set makers will be put out of business if they don't agree to fusion of the two electronic mediums, and the television company CEOs replying in kind.

One of Microsoft's chief allies in this fight, the computer manufacturer Compaq, gave up on the fusion idea in the summer of 1997. At almost the same time, the press began to take notice of a new book by Dr. Michael L. Dertouzos, who has headed the computer laboratory at the Massachusetts Institute of Technology for the past twenty years. The book, called *What Will Be*, laments the complexity of PCs in bold terms. "You want to use them as boat anchors," Dertouzos told the *New York Times*. "People really should revolt." Since many of the most important players in the computer business are former students of Dr. Dertouzos, this pronouncement was not to be taken lightly. In the same article, friend and colleague Dr. Leonard Kleinrock, a computer scientist at the University of California at Los Angeles, pointed a direct finger at Bill Gates, saying, "Anything Microsoft does makes it worse." But other computer scientists say that the complexity prob-

It's important that both the good and bad points of the technological advances be discussed broadly so that society as a whole, rather than just technologists, can guide their direction.

—BILL GATES, 1996

lem can only get worse because both computers and software become outdated before anything gets fixed or simplified.

Bill Gates and other Microsoft executives insist they are working to simplify computer software, but many observers are dubious. In any case, Bill Gates is not about to give up on the idea of merging the personal computer and the television set. In April, Microsoft acquired Web TV Networks Inc., a company specializing in Internet-via-TV services based on set-top boxes, and followed that up in June with a $1 billion investment in the Comcast Corporation, the fourth-ranked television cable company. Such acquisitions and investments put Microsoft in an even stronger position to influence the shape of the emerging information highway. With $9 billion in cash reserves, Microsoft can afford to spend a great deal of money to see to it that Bill Gates's vision of the future comes true.

Over the years, I've been struck by many ways I've seen PC empower people in many walks of life to do great things—things they never dreamed possible. Write a book. Start a business. Communicate with people on continents they may never visit.

Sure, PC empowerment is a grandiose concept. After all, the PC is used as much for playing games and telling multimedia stories as for finding cures for cancer. But most of it is about solving problems, enabling you to learn and augmenting your impact on the world by giving you powerful tools.

—BILL GATES, 1996